Learn Dog with Dog Logic

Maree Hart

Published by Doglogicnz, 2024.

While every precaution has been taken in the preparation of this book, the publisher assumes no responsibility for errors or omissions, or for damages resulting from the use of the information contained herein.

LEARN DOG WITH DOG LOGIC

First edition. August 5, 2024.

ISBN: 979-8224319176

Written by Maree Hart.

SOME SUBJECTS COVERED IN THIS BOOK INCLUDE:

Pulling on the lead

How to get the focus from your dog

Jumping up

Barking

Digging

Not listening

Recall

Aggression

And so much more.....

I suggest you also watch my videos on most social media platforms and that will help you to better understand what you are reading or listening to here.

@doglogicnz

www.doglogictalk.com[1]

Thank You

My editor: my first thank you is to Sue Towler who has helped me bring my writings of a dog training book to fruition. Being an author herself, Sue was able to put my writing, and ideas into a more understandable format. Let's face it, my expertise is speaking dog not writing books.

Sue's writing genre is mainly NZ Historic Fiction and Travel stories, you can check out her website at https://www.suetowler.com.

Book cover: When I reached out to my online community for help with the book cover, Jackie's cover just stood out to me. I explained a bit of what I wanted, and she simply read between the lines and gave me more than I expected. This is not her normal job, Jackie has a wonderful photography business capturing people and their special moments. Please take a look at her stunning work www.jackieophotography.net[1] she is based in Tauranga New Zealand

Audio book: I was so nervous when I first knocked on the door of the Good Boy Music Studio in Mount Maunganui. Keegan Meiring welcomed in me to his studio and I felt relaxed straight away and he made the process so easy. It didn't take too long before we got into the grove of things, and it all began to flow. https://goodboymusic.co.nz[2]

I am so grateful for these wonderful people and the several people that I gave a draft copy of the book to and their comments back. Thank you all so very much for believing in me and supporting this journey to get this book published.

---

1. http://www.jackieophotography.net

2. https://goodboymusic.co.nz/

Introduction

The human element

Let's get something straight right from the start - I am not here to teach your dogs' anything, I am here to train *You* how to communicate with your dog.

Kiss - Keep It Super Simple - is my motto.

It's just about changing *Your* habits around your dog.

A lot of dog training systems fail because you are not sticking with one system long enough or maybe not doing the work regularly enough.

Dog training should become a habit not a chore. There are a lot of wonderful dog trainers out there, you just need to stick to the one system that works for you and don't chop and interchange parts of each system. You need to use ONE system in its entirety, if that doesn't work for you then try another system.

Focus

The focus of this book is about **behavior** not **obedience.**

Behavior is = I Expect this behavior to happen.

Obedience is = You tell them the command each time.

There is an overwhelming amount of information out there so what is different about what I do?

- I use the dog's natural instincts.

- I train the humans to speak dog, I do not try to teach a dog to speak human.

- I like to keep it simple and often get called the 'Dog Whisperer' because of my training methods.

I ask that when you trial my training system 'Dog Logic NZ, that you please use only these methods during the trial. When people use a bit of their own and a bit of another way of training, that is when things often go wrong, and none of it makes any sense to the dog. It takes on average six weeks to change your habits so, if you can commit for that long, you will go a long way towards having a happier, more balanced relationship with your dog.

The methods I use are not new or different. I feel over the years that people have over complicated things, and dog training is no exception. I believe in a more natural, holistic approach to dog training. I prefer to take the fight out of it and get the respect and, as we all know, true respect must be earned and not forced.

What I do Not use is pinch collars, electric collars, treat training, alpha holds or anything that will make you fight or hurt your dog. This is not a necessary way of training. A dog in fear will never have a healthy respect for you.

Why I do not use treat training as my main tool:

I know of far too many dogs that have bitten because of food aggression. If you are always giving treats, it can take away the natural instinct for the dog to look at you for safety and that is the goal here, you cannot bribe safety and trust.

If you give your dog permission to eat food from anyone's hand, including a small child's, this is an unsafe action. I do not believe in bribing for behavior, I prefer to use respect, as that is the goal for any training with a dog. What happens if you have no treats?

There are a few trainers out there who are telling you to starve a dog before a lesson; you are kidding me right? Dogs will only learn that they get more high value treats when they hold out for something better. 'Oops I fed my dog, now I can't do any training with it', and the list goes on and on. So please, when using the **Dog Logic NZ** system, **Do Not** use any treat training, as you will then have to untrain the treat training to get the true respect back.

The first exercise I like to do is *Attentiveness training*. As with all my behavior training, no treats are required. I am not saying that treat training is bad, not at all, I just feel it doesn't fit with behavior training, but it is ok for obedience and agility training etc.

I won't go into the studies I have done, the courses I have completed and the thousands of hours of research I have put in, because I want this book to be easy to understand and to make dog training as simple as possible by using the KISS method - Keep It Super Simple. Be kind and the training will go well

Life stages of your dog

Dogs go through stages in life just like people do, and each time they go through a stage you will have to take a step back, look at what's happening, and start from the beginning again. The dog needs to be reminded that you are running the show and that they are safe and you have their back. An example of those stages would be:

- A Toddler - 3 to 6 months, no ears and full of mischief, just wants to explore and try everything out because the world is all so new.
- A Tweenager - 6 to 12 months, basically just a pain in the ass, trying to be a teenager with a child's mind.

- The Teenager - 12 to 18 months, Oh dear, they know it all and think they can be an adult who knows better than you do.
- Then, just when you thought you had everything sorted, you get the senior. At about 7 years old your dog turns 50, this is when you get the 'I don't give a shit' and 'do not mess with me' attitudes. These times vary depending on a variety of things; the work you have done, the breed of the dog and other environmental and genetic reasons.

First Assessment Sheet

Before you start your training, I would like you to fill in this behavior assessment. I do not expect you to understand or even score any of these things higher than a 2. This sheet is useful for two reasons, first so you have some goals to set yourself with your dog training and second, so you can monitor your progress as you work through this training. There are more sheets throughout the book so you can check on your progress. Have fun.

Dog's Name: Age:

Breed: Today's Date:

How to rate your dog's progress:

ACHIEVEMENT LEVEL	SCORE
Absolutely Wonderful, no improvement required	5
Best efforts, just about there	4
Could have been better, understanding just no follow through	3
Did try, well ok needs to try harder	2
Effort was not really there	1
Forget it, epic fail. Come on human I do not understand	0

Dog's Training - score 1 to 5 for each action - with 5 being the highest score

ACTION   **SCORE**

Do I look at my human's face when there is trouble or I am afraid

How is my short lead work at home

How is my short lead walk out with distractions

How is my long lead work at home

How is my long lead walk out with distractions

Putting the lead on calmly

What am I like around my human's food

Is my barking a problem

My obedience commands. down- stay- wait

How is my mat and/or crate training going

Am I doing well when guests arrive

Recall at home

Recall out in public with distractions

Boundary work, keep out of the kitchen, don't go out of the gate

Respond to the word "Leave"

Dog reactive

People Reactive

My reaction to loud noises

Obsessive behavior

Separation Anxiety

Vet Check by my human

Vet check by the vet

Nail clipping

Total Score

   Human Training Self Check - Score 1 to 5 for each action - 5 being the highest score

ACTION   **SCORE**

Has my human done attentiveness training at least 3 times a day

Has my human praised me enough

Has my human taken me for a walk each day

Has my human seen how my focus is casually around the home

Has my human set up distraction training often enough

How is my human's breathing and calm while training

Is my human making more rules for me and sticking to them

Is my human being consistent with my training

Is my human using their emotions with their commands

Total Score

Attentiveness Training

This is the most important chapter of the book! If you read this and nothing else, your dog's behaviour will improve greatly as will your approach towards your dog training. This is the key to my system – the Dog Logic NZ system.

To put it in a nutshell - Attentiveness Training is:

- On a lead
- Call your dog
- Praise when it looks at you
- Growl and a snap on the lead when it goes to walk away
- Praise and smile when it looks back at you.

Dog Logic's Attentiveness Training - what is it?

It is all about communicating with your dog in a way the dog understands. There is no point in going against the dog's natural way of behaving.

A pack leader doesn't give the omega dog a treat for doing the right thing, it gives it a good accepting energy, and the main principles of survival which are:

- Food
- Shelter
- Safety
- Respect,
- Care and
- Pack security

The dog needs to understand that it will also receive this from us. This is the primary goal of the **Dog Logic NZ** training system.

Training is all about *growl* and *praise*. Let them know what is wrong and what is right.

Wrong is uncomfortable, right is comfortable.

Growl then praise = Focus Trust and Respect

Dogs use these four different levels of communication in this order.

1) The body language – Keep your body tall when telling them off. You will notice a dog will have their tail and shoulders up.

2) The growl, or voice – Avoid the word No – Use Ar-r-r-rt, or something that sounds like a growl, sometimes your dog will have a silent growl and just flick it's lip up in a snarl.

3) The snap – Distraction such as a flick up on the lead, clap your hands or stamp your foot. The dog's snap is a close bite with normally no connection as it is a warning.

4) The bite – No hitting, (or biting from their point of view), required as this shows you are weak.

The value of a growl and a praise

There are different levels of praise. When you overpay, your dog it will not be bothered working again for you that day. If you underpay, they will feel it is not worth their while listening to you.

One dollar praise is a low-level praise - this is a:

'That was okay but you really could do a bit better, but I am happy with you, good dog,'

a quiet level of praise and give them a smile.

Twenty-dollar praise is normal everyday praise and this is what most of it should be.

This is simply; '*Good Dog*' in a normal, kind, happy tone with a big smile.

Remember Not to say 'good dog, good dog, good dog' over and over again, nag, nag, nag, just say it once. You want your dog to want the praise, not get sick of it. Make sure you have a good happy emotion attached to this praise.

Hundred-dollar praise 'GOOD DOG, YES'. This one is huge praise for things like recall, stopping barking at that cat on the fence etc. For example, when first doing the Attentiveness training, it is a big deal when the dog first looks at you, that is worthy of a big hundred-dollar praise, but when the dog has turned away a little and then turned back, a one-dollar praise is sufficient. Many people will over praise and growl and eventually it will just become nagging and white noise to the dog. Do not overuse.

My dog doesn't react to my praise:

This is because you have overused praise. Let's go back to the beginning, when you are giving your dog some gentle love, say the words 'good dog'. This will let them know that the words 'good dog', 'good boy/girl ' or 'good (name)' is praise, and this will bring trust. Please use good/happy energy because they respond to energy.

Stop, Breathe and take control:

It is so important with this training that we *breathe*, and not just from our chest. You need to go deep into your stomach and take a full belly breath. If you are not the best at breathing, as many of us aren't, try downloading a breathing App and learn how to breathe correctly. Sit with your dog at least once a day for a full minute and just practise your breathing. This is great for calming yourself and at the same time bringing a closer connection with your dog.

How to do Attentiveness training: The Key to the Dog Logic System

Have your dog on a lead, it should be no shorter than two metres long, with a collar or non-restricting harness. A collar is the best option as a harness can often encourage a dog to pull.

For this exercise, make sure you stand in one place. If your dog moves around or behind you, stand your ground, do not move towards the dog. Dogs often try to get you to turn around, so please do Not move your feet. Make sure you do not use any obedience commands like, sit, stay, heel etc. This is a *behaviour* exercise not an *obedience* one.

Take a deep breath, smile and relax.

Call your dog to you in a nice, kind tone. If the dog looks at you, Praise and smile. Often at this stage the dog will try to avoid eye contact as they are trying to keep the control. Take it slow and stay calm, you need that eye contact, do not stare when you get it, just smile, praise and look away. Staring at your dog can cause them to think you want to challenge them.

When your dog walks away or looks away, do a low guttural growl, Ar-r-r-rt. Praise as soon as it looks at you. They do not need to keep looking at you, but they should not move away. The goal here is to get your dog to look at you and stay close, it doesn't have to keep looking at you but it can't move away.

The Look - this is when they finally look at you and lick their lips. They will then relax and that is the sign of them trusting you and not trying to "Take control".

Next time the dog moves or looks away, growl and snap the lead at the same time. Praise for *the look*. If you get frustrated at any time you must stop and breathe. Do not pat or physically touch your dog during this exercise, you want it to learn that a praise close up or from a distance is enough of a reward. Once the exercise is complete you can then calmly stroke your dog.

We need your dog to have some mouth movement here such as licking of the lips or a yawn. When people say licking of the lips is anxiety, I agree to a point, it is more like saying I am sorry. The dog will feel that way when it is saying sorry just before it becomes calm. If your dog does not look at you and licks its lips, or you don't have mouth movement, it is not taking this seriously and the Attentiveness training will *Not* hold. Your dog best be sorry for not listening and giving you focus. After the lick of the lips, your dog will then relax. Take a deep breath with your dog and smile at it. Seeing and feeling the difference of that focus, it is so beautiful, it is one of the most beautiful moments you will ever have with your dog, the connection is an incredible feeling. This is when your dog fully clicks into you, you will feel the difference.

Keep it simple in order to get the look and mouth movement. Use the dog's name - praise if they look at you or growl and snap the lead if they don't, and then repeat until they click into you. Clicking into you is the feeling of connection and the dog listening and trying to understand you.

Once you succeed at this exercise you can then do it off lead. You say the dog's name, it looks at you, you praise it – yes, it's that simple. If you can do this ten times a day, wow think of the focus and trust you will get then. Effort = Results. If you do this once a day you will get results in a few months. If you commit to this training exercise for the next six weeks, three to ten times a day, Wow the results will be outstanding.

When I have a new 'Train and Board', I will do this exercise up to thirty times a day in the first three to five days.

When you go to a new place and you need your dog's attention, get out of the car and do the Attentiveness training. This lets your dog know that while you are here, in this place, it is safe and you have control of the situation.

Don't do this exercise, or any of them, in the same place and at the same time every day. Mix it up a little or it will become an obedience exercise. Don't do this exercise when you are stressed or pissed off with your dog, you need to control your energy with this or it will all go wrong.

The points system:

As with everything in life, people, dogs and other lifeforms, we are all working for points in our relationships. It could be at work, it could be with your children or partner, there is a reason for everything we do. It is not a bad thing, it just is what it is. You make your partner, boss, workmate a cup of coffee, why? Because you want to earn a point and that point could just be to show them you are a nice person or it could be as simple as you wanting to be noticed, acknowledged, or you're working for that promotion, or you want an extra cuddle. This is no different with dogs. Our goal here is to take the pressure off your dog. If your dog is not always having to earn points it can relax more.

So how do we lose points with them?

1. They come to you and demand a pat and you pat them - oops you lost that point.

2. They tell you to open the door - darn another point gone (you need to wait a few moments and then let them out when they are not TELLING you to let them out).

3. They jump up on you. This is a big one. If you just slightly turn away you can get the win back, if you hit them or push them down you lose several points.

4. Pulling on the lead, loads of points lost here.
5. Jumping on your knee without invitation, more points lost.

6. Jumping on the bed or chair without being invited. They own the bed if they get in first. I do not mind dogs sleeping with their humans however, it must only be by invitation and if they do not have separation anxiety. (Read the chapter on Separation Anxiety).

Anything where your dog demands you to do anything, you are losing points.

I work on the pack system, as we all do. It might be your siblings, parents, partner or your boss. We all work on the pack system, birds, cows, horses, and dogs are no different. Often one person is the pack leader in the kitchen but might not be the leader in the backyard. We feel safe in any relationship when we know where we stand, it is no different for dogs. If they feel that you are in control, they become a better protector, they want to do more for you. They feel safer when they are with you. And when you go away from them, they have less stress in their world as they know their pack leader has put them somewhere safe.

A lot of trainers are saying that the pack system is outdated, well hang on a minute. The pack or the family, or the herd, or the flock, everything in our world, be it animal or human, has leadership. Now if there's nobody in charge, things can tend to get a little bit chaotic. You don't have to have someone who is a lot higher up but there is always someone who is going to be that little bit higher than everybody else. Take a classroom full of students for example, you have a teacher who is the pack leader. Now, if that teacher does not have control over those students, they are going to be a real pain in the you-know-what. They are going to be disruptive and they are not going to listen and learn. However, if that teacher has got leadership and the respect of the class, everyone will feel safe, just the same as if it was the head of your household. Whatever the situation, there is always a pack leader. Wolf packs, dogs, chickens, even a house full of cats, there is always going to be a boss or pack leader. There's nothing wrong with having a pack system. The whole point of a pack system is to make everyone feel safe, loved and respected.

Sandy with Cobba's Lesson

A lady turned up to my dog training centre and her two little dogs were barking in the car. It was sad, it kinda breaks my heart a little when I hear that sort of behaviour as I know the dogs are doing it out of stress. Sandy was apologetic and said, 'they always do that'. I explained to her that the stress that they were feeling at having to bark at this new problem, this new place, was too much for them.

Sandy had been training agility and scent-work dogs for years and she was amazing with her dogs. They were so well cared for and very obedient, it was beautiful. One of her dogs was so stressed with life that it would spin in circles, very similar to when dogs go kennel mad or catching air. These dogs all have one thing in common, they do not have strong pack leadership and often do not have enough to do - in the form of daily jobs. In this case it was the pack leadership.

I noted that while Sandy had nine-year-old Cobba out of the car, Cobba was very stressed, spinning and barking at seemingly nothing. Cobba did not once look at Sandy for guidance. This told me that Cobba was taking on all the responsibility of the surroundings, it was being the pack leader. This poor wee thing had no idea how to control this new place, the new noises, new people, everything was far too overwhelming.

I asked Sandy to hand me her dog (it was important she walk towards me and hand the dog over so the dog understands that it is ok with this new person). If I walked towards Sandy and took the dog from her, that is threatening, so not advisable.

I did the Attentiveness training with Cobba, it only took about 5 minutes and Cobba just looked at me and started to relax. Each time he barked or looked stressed at a noise; I did a low growl followed by a quick praise. Cobba started to look at me without me asking, so he always got a praise. Now, with all those noises going on around us, Cobba would look at me for guidance. Once I showed him (by not reacting) that there was no threat, he would once again relax. If he did react out of fear or concern, I did another low growl and praise. The praise is so important here as we do not want to frighten or make the dog more timid. (Read Sympathy Causes Fear). My breathing and calm at this time was also very important.

We went to another part of the property to test how he would respond. We took the other dog with us and Cobba just looked at me. I smiled with a calming energy and that told him he was safe, so he relaxed. In the meantime the other dog was pacing around as we had not done any Attentiveness training with that one.

I got a call from Sandy a week later to say the barking and spinning had stopped, she was in tears of gratitude. Pack leadership works.

John and Remmi's Lesson

Remmi is a Gorden Setter, a beautiful dog with boundless energy. They came into the Pet Lodge and after the first stay I said I would love them to do a lesson with me as this dog had no 'ears'. He would not look at me and he would not listen to anything I said. John was using Remmi as his running mate and had done so since before he was even a year old. This dog was huge, so firstly I was concerned that he had too much energy and second, that he would start having sore bones very early in life.

A giant or large breed like Remmi should not be run this hard. John described his dog as a mental nutcase and out of control. John said he was not at all interested in doing a lesson as they'd had three different trainers in the past and had spent thousands of dollars and could not see any results. What I could see was that either John had not done the work that he was taught by the trainers or, the system they used with him was not working for Remmi or the humans. All three trainers had used treat training on Remmi and this dog was not interested in food, so all the trainers told him to get high value treats like cheese, sausage etc and starve him before the lesson. John was told he could only train this dog while he was hungry. My head was spinning with disbelief at this stage, but John was still not interested in a lesson. So I invited them to come to my next stage show, and he and his wife did.

The next weekend Remmi came to stay at my Pet Lodge, wow what a difference. He looked straight at me and made full eye contact. He had never stayed still long enough to look like that before. They had decided not to run him so hard and halved his run so he wasn't so over fit. Even after one week he was starting to settle. John was so excited they had found a simple system that he gave me a Hi-five and leapt in the air. I must say I have never had that response from a client before. It just filled my heart to know Remmi was not going to live in confusion and frustration anymore. This dog, if he was a human, I would say he was ADHD so working with this dog was harder than most.

Communication

Sit - Stop it - shut up- get down - piss off - No - OK

Get off the damn chair

Get out of that room

Pushing - pulling - fighting and not for play

Grabbing at the dog

Smothering - scooping up off the ground.

We use far too many useless, unhelpful words or actions.

Let's stop over-complicating things, we *need* to keep things simple and easy for the dog to understand. Remember the KISS method - *Keep It Super Simple*.

For this to work effectively you must use your calm and your breathing techniques to earn the trust of your dog. You will not be able to take any of these steps when you or your dog are in a state of panic, anger, sorrow or fear. For your dog to learn, you must be in a state of calm. To achieve this I suggest you do some breathing exercises with your dog, feel the safety and the trust that you hold together. Never work with your dog when you are rushing or in the wrong state of mind. Fake happy, calm, brave, if you have to and read the **Find my Brave** chapter first.

Body Language

This could be a book on its own, so I will write in simple terms as I am wanting to keep the work relatable.

The four main things we use to train dogs is: our body language, voice, snap and our praise.

Dogs use these four different levels of communication in this order:

1) The body language – Keep your body tall when telling them off, lower when calling and for Praise

2) The growl, or voice – Avoid the word 'No' – Use *Ar-r-r-rt*, or something that sounds like a growl, as this is something the dog understands. Praise

3) The snap – Distraction such as a flick on the lead, clap your hands or stamp your foot. Praise

4) The bite – Do not use this method of communication as it shows you are weak. Hitting or Slapping is 'biting' in dog language. Hitting shows you are weak. No. Also, no grabbing their collar in anger. Praise is the most important thing here

It is important to understand these four levels of communication, as that is the way dogs understand what you are asking of them. And remember, there must be *praise* at each level.

Body language is the only universal language there is.

The Praise

When you praise your dog, use a friendly tone. If you don't find that easy, smile when you are saying it. This might sound silly, but it works. Don't forget to praise when they are doing well, praise is their payment. Make sure you don't underpay or overpay. There is small, medium and large praise, depending on the severity of the growl used. Small growl small praise, medium growl medium praise, and large growl large praise.

This is how you program your dog to the praise. When you are giving your dog gentle loving pats, say good dog, smile, feel the love and the closeness. They will feel this when you are working with them while they are doing the work. If you pat your dog hard while praising, you could be hurting them and they will not respond as well to the praise.

The Growl

When you growl at them, use a guttural deep word or sound. *Arrrt* is what I use as it has a natural growl to it. Never growl their name though! Their name is all about love and praise, if you use it in a growl tone, they will not respond well when you call their name.

Make sure you do not over growl when they are reacting as this can put everything into over excitement or even a panic state and no one learns in that state. Stop and breathe, clear your mind, *feel* the focus and connection between you and your dog.

The Snap

I use the lead while training. Snap the lead up just like a dog would snap its mouth towards another dog. This snap could be many things, you could use a sound like a clap of your hands. You could use a plastic jar with stones in it. You could use a water pistol or water bombs when outside, or just use their lead, anything to distract them from what they are doing wrong. This will let them know we are serious.

Don't forget to praise. Praise – Praise – Praise, it lets them know they are doing the right thing. Praise is the payment and the goal.

The Bite

You never need to hit your dog!!! This will teach them to bite. Aggression builds aggression. Often when a dog is hit or reprimanded aggressively, they might not bite you but they will bite or hurt others.

Each time you do something with your hands on the dog, it is like them using their mouths. As we know, they don't have hands so they think 'mouth'. If we hit them, in their minds we are biting them, if we pat/stroke them we are grooming them.

In short, Growl for behavior you don't want, and Praise for the good behavior you do want. Comfortable Vs Uncomfortable.

Timing

If you get the timing wrong by even a split second, you can cause more problems than before. If the timing is wrong the training will not work. By giving praise when a dog is looking at the problem, that's telling the dog that the problem behavior is okay. If you growl when the dog has stopped reacting, they will think they are doing something wrong.

Praise for good - Growl for unwanted behavior

Commands

You must keep your commands simple. Dogs cannot hold as many words in their vocabulary as us so use them wisely. Some researchers say dogs have 70 to 120 words, others say around 200, so let's not over complicate life and keep it simple.

No = don't do that, stop it, shut up, piss off, #@#&, get down etc etc, blah blah blah, too many words.

There are many alternatives for the word 'No' and we should not use the word No anyway as it is too common. No is used in many conversations and yelled a lot so your dog becomes desensitized to it. Do you want a coffee? NO THANKS, do you KNOW how often that word is used every day... NO I don't. OK so you get the point here, please do not use common words as commands.

Replace NO with - *Arrrrtt*

Replace OK as your release word, with an uncommon word like Zip - Free - Jip - Cross, or just make up some random word as a release word. Please do not use the word OK as a release word, it is used far too often in everyday conversations.

There are only two harsh words the dog should hear from you - '*Arrrrt*' and '*Leave*'.

'*Arrrrt*' is good for everything you want to say '*No*' to, every behavior you do not like. '*Leave*' is a good serious word for situations such as looking at food on the table or looking at that cat or another dog you don't want them to meet. Tone is very important here. When it is a praise, it must be a happy tone, when it is a *growl* or *leave,* use a guttural tone.

DO NOT ever growl their name. If you growled MAREE to me I would not have any respect for you or want to listen to you. The dog's name must be said with pure love and even better, with a smile.

With the voice we hear words, whereas the dog will hear 'tones' first. You could say the same word with three different tones and they will hear three different commands. When giving them a command, use your normal voice, make sure you say it clearly and do not repeat it.

Energy

When using your commands, it is important that you *feel* what you are saying. You have to be serious about what you say. Dogs feel your vibration, that is largely how they communicate, like a sixth sense. When I want to work on the 'crossing the road' exercise, I picture a dog getting hit by a car so that when I growl just as they are about to go on the road, my whole body *feels* the dog getting hit just as it is about to step onto the road, so my Growl *Ar-r-r-r-t* is serious. It has fear and an energy spike to it and they can feel that. I don't need to have that picture in my head anymore because now I can reach that feeling automatically, however sometimes when I get a dog that is really hard to work with, I have to put that picture back in my head just so I can get that feeling deeper in my body.

This works for the praise as well, you must *feel* happy, pleased, excited that they have done well. If there is no emotion or energy behind those words, there is no point in saying them as the dog will not believe you.

If you do not use energy to back up your words it will take you a lot longer to train your dog for anything, and they will know you are not serious. Practice your Red flag and Green flag exercises daily in the early stages to make this easier, this comes up a little later in the book.

Lesson - Dog Trainers

When I train people who want to be dog trainers, one of my favourite days is when we go to the pound or animal rescue and get them to bring out dogs that are not easy to handle. Then I get these new trainers to do the Attentiveness training and simple lead work with them. They are told before the dogs come out, that they are not to say anything, no words, no commands, no voice at all, the dog is not to hear their voice. Why, because it is important when you use the Dog Logic NZ training system that you understand how to use your ENERGY to communicate.

On this particular occasion I had three trainers with me. One of them, Kathren, had this over-excitable Terrier given to her by the animal rescue staff. And yes, as we know, most Terriers are very excitable. Kathren started to ask me a question so I got the masking tape from my pocket and told her that if she wanted to ask me a question or talk to the dog then the masking tape would go on. Yes, I *felt* it when I said it to her. Point taken, she just smiled at me and shut her mouth. I instructed that due to the breed of the dog, the lead focus work would be best done before the Attentiveness training. Kathren's energy was all over the place, frustrated, so I said – 'just stop and breathe, calm the dog with your breath and your energy first'. This dog started to slow down, stopped jumping up and then after a few minutes just looked at her. Kathren had the biggest smile and felt so excited and pleased the dog just wanted to keep looking at her for that feeling. About five minutes later Kathren was able to do the Attentiveness training with the same result. This was the most beautiful thing to watch. You could see the dog was not used to feeling safe or protected and now it had a pack leader and it just melted. It was one of those moments that was so special to watch, I now use it as one of my green flags.

I looked around and the staff from the rescue centre and the other trainers were all in shock, some even had tears in their eyes. They could not believe the transformation in this dog that no one could handle without a battle. Kathren had done it with no words and using just her energy. I don't suggest you try this until you have a lot more training with your words and body language first, Kathren had been working with me in a live-in, full time training situation for two weeks at this stage.

Kathren saved that dog from being put to death just by using that bit of training and understanding, it was due to be put down the next day along with several others.

Passive Dominance Vs Assertive Dominance

The word dominance in dog training, I feel, has been misused. The old school training was all about the Alpha hold, this was pushing your dog to the ground and holding it down until it stopped fighting.... DO NOT DO THIS. The likelihood of you getting attacked by your dog is huge and let's be real, if you tried to hold me down, I would damn well bite you and you would deserve it. You do Not need to fight with your dog, that is why we are getting so many dogs attacking people now.

Assertive dominance is just about the growl, snap and using your strong body language, voice tones, and assertive energy. If you soften your body language and lower yourself, you are in a submissive position. Your dog will take advantage of that until it understands that *You* are the pack leader.

Passive dominance is the higher form of Dominance. This is where you use calm controlled body language, ignoring behavior you do not want, using a low guttural growl, not a loud and assertive one. When your dog is on lead, just calmly walk in a different direction and praise when they come with you. Passive dominance is calm, precise and controlled. You need to work *with* your dog's nature, not try and humanize it.

If it upsets you, don't use the word dominance, just say Uncomfortable vs Comfortable.

The leader always leads, doesn't it? Isn't this just good manners?

This is another passive way to earn points with your dog. Walking through a door first, leading the way upstairs, places where your dog rushes out in front of you, this is where you can, in a passive way, earn points. If your dog rushes out in front of you just turn around and go the other way, then come back and try again. Each time your dog runs past you, just stop and get ready to turn again. Once the dog stops and looks at you before running through the door, *praise it*. The goal is to walk through the door and for the dog to decide on its own that it is best to let you go first. All these small passive dominant exercises earn you a lot of points with quiet and calm. Yes, you can do the same exercise on lead with the growl and praise. Often for the more serious areas, such as the front door out to the road, this is where I would have them on a lead, it is more assertive dominance.

I have no problem when my dogs' walk-in front of me in some places, but if your dog is always in front, how is it looking at you for guidance? *They* are taking on the walk and all the pressure of everything going on around them, if they are not checking in with you.

You often get a passively dominant dog that is always in the lead but it never causes problems at home, why is this? Well, because it knows what points to let go with you. It understands that doing the things that you want is easier than the battle or the fight.

The point of this is that your dog needs to feel safe and understand where it stands in the pack or family.

The difference between behavior training and obedience training

Simply put, behavior is *expected*, it is not an *obedience* command. I *Expect* that behavior every time, end of story. I should not have to tell the dog each time. Obedience is a command said each time.

Examples of expected behavior:

- boundary work
- they are never to come into the kitchen
- they can never jump out of the car without the release word
- they are never to cross a road without a release word

These are all examples of *expected* behavior.

Be aware that behavior can also be a temperament.

Let me explain. When you have a dog with behavioral issues such as ADHD and bi-polar, their behavior is due to their temperament. And yes such human behaviors do exist in dogs, this has been widely studied and proven. This does not give you an excuse to put up with unwanted behaviors though. 'My dog is on the spectrum so it can do that' - NO it can't.

You can also expect different behavioral patterns from working dogs such as huntaways, border collies, hunting dogs, jack russel's and foxies. If you put these dogs in a docile, non-working, domestic environment, of course you are going to have behavioral issues to deal with. This is not ADHD. For instance, foxies have a very high prey-drive so they are naturally going to go nuts over chasing a ball or anything else that they can chase. Stop using the excuse that 'my dog is on the spectrum or, it is a typical Terrier so it can get away with bad behavior'.

Obedience is a command or action that you have to say each time - Such as - *Sit, stay, heel, wait,* for example.

I would also put the likes of tricks and agility in this heading. Yes, most of these things are great to teach your dog, however, obedience will not fix a behavior problem. I have no problem with people using treats to achieve these results.

Let's talk about treats for a minute. Treats can cause food obsession or aggression. Some dogs are food focused; some are not. What is stopping a dog from grabbing food from a child's hand when you have previously told the dog it is ok to take food from an adult's hand? Many dogs will drool when they look at food, what an unnecessary mess. Just use fun and praise and you will get a better result in the long run.

How to let my dog on the couch by invitation?

If your dog jumps on the couch and you have missed the signs before they jump up, then you will have to get up and call them off the couch. You should growl *before* they jump up, not after. If they do not come, do not grab their collar as that is aggressive, you must get a slip lead or loop the handle of your lead, then gently pull them off the couch and as soon as their paws hit the floor - Praise - saying *off or down* as you are pulling them down. As they get to jump up again, growl before they get up and praise them for not jumping up. For at least 24 hours they are Not allowed up on the couch or chair until they learn it is only by invitation that they can jump up. This is the same for your bed, they should NEVER be the first one on your bed. I have no problem if you want your dog to sleep with you, however this must be by invitation only, otherwise they will own the bed.

What new rules and behaviors will you make for your dog?

Everyone must be on the same page with your dog's new rules as it is not fair that the rules are one thing for one person and a different rule for another, this is just confusing as it sets them up to get into trouble. I suggest you make a list so that everyone in the house can see the new rules.

Not to get on the couch or bed without an invitation
Stay out of the kitchen

Breathing and calm

There is no point in trying to work with your dog if you are angry, sad, or the world feels just too daunting. In saying that, dog training can help to ground you once you know how to do it right. While you are learning these exercises, it is better to be in a good frame of mind.

When you say something with meaning, it holds and projects energy, we all know this. If you look at someone and feel and say, I love you, the other person feels it too. If you say I am very angry with you, they will also feel that. Dogs may not understand exactly the same way as we do, however they do feel the difference between happy, pleased, angry, cross and other emotions. That is why breathing and calm is so very important. Dogs can read people better than people can read people.

Case in point:

We had a little staffy-labrador-cross in the Pet Lodge for about four or five days and the first day she was here she was literally throwing her body at the front of her bedroom. She was digging holes, she was biting the wire, her anxiety was huge. Her humans had previously done a training session with me but they had held on to the growl side of things rather than using *calm and breathing and Praise*. So what happened was, they were winding themselves up, which in turn was winding the dog up. They were fighting with this dog. She was a sweet girl but so full of anxiety. She was empathic, which means she would take on people's emotions. When you got cross or angry with her or portrayed any high energy emotions or excited energy, she would take that on as well.

The *only* way to work with a dog like this is to work with her on a long lead, breathe - and calm down. Lean down to pat her, then as soon as she starts to get wound up stand up, turn away from her, and breathe. Praise her as soon she gets down, soft, gentle praise. High energy praise is not going to work, an excited pat will not work, treat training will not work. You need to just *calm*, take a breath and *slow*. Every time you get angry with this dog she is going to leap around; she is going to go outside and dig holes and rip up everything. She will destroy your garden; she will destroy your house. The only way to deal with this beautiful dog is to calm yourself so she too can learn to calm herself.

When you've had a hard day at work, or you are angry or wound up about something, - *do not* work with your dog. It doesn't have to be anything to do with your dog that has pissed you off or upset you, life just happens. Pull your head in, go back, do your breathing and calm exercises, and then work with your dog - or don't.

I will often walk into a home and the energy is all over the place, people have had enough of the dog's behaviour and they are simply "over it". Confusion and frustration causes our energy to spike. We can learn to control this by changing our mood and our energy and most importantly, our mindset. Dogs communicate a lot through energy and body language cues. Try it, convince yourself that you are happy. Don't say anything, just feel happy, smile, feel the energy going through your body and walk around slowly with your dog. Keep thinking of something that makes you feel really happy. Watch your dog, they will be happy too and they will often ask you to play using the play bow, or just want to be with you.

Take a break and do a couple of minutes of relaxing breathing, find your inner calm. Deep breathing can also relax your dog. I do this with every dog I work with. It is the first thing I do when I start working with a dog because if my breathing and energy is all over the place so will theirs be and they will not understand what I want from them.

Now, try being very cross or disappointed. Feel it, think of something that makes you cross. Look at your dog, but don't stare, never stare at your dog as you don't want to challenge it. Walk slowly around being grumpy and watch your dog's behaviour. You will notice they will mirror you with their energy.

If you work with your dog before you calm yourself you are setting yourself up to fail, train for success, not to fail. Always end on a happy fun note. You want your dog to *want* to work with you.

Lesson: Helena with Bongo

I answered the phone and a very stressed lady said, 'I love my dog but he is so naughty he does nothing right, he runs away all the time. He jumps all over people and when I leave him he screams and destroys the house. I need to rehome him but he is so bad nobody would want him, so I tried to get him put to sleep because he is such a bad dog. I took him to the vet to get him put to sleep but the vet said I had to see you first'.

I love calls like this. I made the appointment for as soon as I could. The panic in Helena's voice was devastating and there was an urgency about it as she had just returned from the vet.

They arrived at the training room with Bongo pulling Helena up the stairs so hard she could hardly hold him. He was a little blue staffy, a cute wee lad, only two years old. Helena had had Bongo since he was six weeks old, this was too young to be taken from his mother. This often causes separation anxiety and neediness in a dog and this particular breed is often known for its neediness.

'See, he is always this excited about everything, he won't stop, it's like he never sleeps, he's into everything.'

Bongo was going crazy, in a mad panic. Helena's breathing was all over the place and the energy was enough to light up a darn stadium. I asked her to hand me Bongo. I did the Attentiveness training, I needed calm in the room. This behaviour from both of them was madness, a panic.

I normally don't work with a dog until I have explained what I am about to do, but this situation was out of control and there is no way either of them would listen or take any information in. It took about ten minutes to calm Bongo, to get his focus on me, it was really hard. Then it happened - he stopped, looked, licked his lips and yawned. We both took the biggest breath and then he just laid down and relaxed. The shock on Helena's face was beautiful.

"What the hell did you just do to my dog?" she gasped, "he has never been this calm with other people around, and certainly not in a strange place'.

It was at this moment that I could see the trauma in Helena. This dog was never going to be calm with her until she had dealt with her own traumas or learned to *fake her brave*. When she was working with Bongo, she needed to learn how to fake being brave. I explained that when we hang on to our traumas and don't work on them, they stay active within our system and dogs can feel it and they do not understand. Dogs will let go of their traumas, if we let them. That is why I get annoyed when people say, "my dog is a rescue and that is why it is like this". Bullshit, *you* are the reason your dog is still holding the trauma. Either you are holding your own trauma close to the surface, or you keep feeling sorry for the dog because you feel sorry for yourself. Dogs are a great reflection on how we feel and behave. I needed to change Helena's behaviour in order to help Bongo.

I explained to Helena that I could see she had at some stage been traumatised and was holding on to it. I could not see what the trauma was and I did not want or need to know, I am not a people therapist, but I needed to help her *Find her Brave*. You can look at it as - *fake it till you make it*. (I am working on the **Find My Brave** book next.)

We needed to start with her breathing by using an exercise called Red flag/Green flag (I will explain this at the end of this story). I explained to her that because of what she had been through and the way she reflected it, Bongo was picking up on it and didn't understand what she was trying to teach him. The anxiety she felt in certain situations was being reflected on him and he was not coping with the responsibility of it. This is where you need to *find your brave*.

I explained to her that I understood as I have CPTSD (Complex Post-Traumatic Stress Disorder) and I still get overwhelmed and have panic attacks. That's when dogs help me come out of it, because I need to be *brave* for them. I need to *Find my Brave,* or at least fake it.

For the next twenty minutes I worked with Helena on her Red and Green flags and taught her how to breathe. Then and only then, could we work with Bongo.

I stood up and got her to breathe and handed Bongo over to her. He started to get wound up again so I asked her to just stand still and think of her Green flag. She was calm and Bongo looked at her confused then just relaxed, it was beautiful.

We did the Attentiveness training, and her comment was, "you made this exercise look simple, but it is hard'. My answer was, 'Yes, I get that comment a lot, although it will become easier for you with a lot of practice. Keep watching my videos and read your notes often, this is a whole new language for you to learn. I train people, not dogs. Once people understand this system the dogs feel safe and understand what you are trying to say.'

Two weeks later I get a video of her walking Bongo down the street on a loose lead. Bongo's focus was clearly on Helena. The title of her video was, *My calm self with my calm dog loving our new life together.* 'Thank you Maree for changing our lives, I feel so much safer now and braver than I ever have'.

Me with Fee and Binty

When I was a little girl, I used to hide from people. I would go off down the farm with a dog, goat or whatever animal was around, and they would all follow me and do everything I asked of them. I remember this one time I had a dog and a goat with me, Fee and Binty. I had taught them to lay down with me in the grass and, on this occasion, I could hear someone coming and as was my usual practice, I did not want to be found. I took a breath, lay down in the long grass and I felt them laying down beside me. They responded to how I felt, that is how I got them to get down and lay beside me and keep still. I had the picture of stillness and calm in my head. I could feel their breath just as they could feel mine, through our shared energy. The three of us just lay there waiting for the person to leave and as soon as I couldn't hear them anymore, I sat up a little to make sure they were gone. I smiled and changed my energy to fun and the three of us stood up and carried on playing.

This is a great tool for when you are having problems calming your dog. Hold the handle of the lead, sit on a chair and breathe, do not touch your dog. Picture yourself lightly stroking your dog but do not physically do it. Be calm and picture their calm. Breathe in through your nose and out through your mouth. The first time you do this with your dog they will be a little confused, so only do it for two or three minutes to start with. Feel the energy, the calm, the love you have with that dog. You can do it in a closed room instead of using a lead if you prefer.

Red flag Green flag exercise:

This exercise can help you to change your mood or mindset when you are wanting to work with your dog but you really don't feel like it. I refer to this a lot in the book, I find it a very useful tool when I need to quickly switch into a better frame of mind.

Red Flag: Think of something not so nice, something that makes you feel uncomfortable, that's your Red Flag. For me it could be going to a mall or getting overwhelmed by doing my business accounts. Where do you feel that in your body? Chest, tummy or all over? Hold that feeling for a few moments. It is good to recognize this feeling so that we don't just walk around with this being our default mood. You will be surprised how often we do that.

Green Flag*:* Now think of something that warms your heart and makes you smile, it could be something that was a special moment in your life, the first time you stood on top of a mountain, the first time you got off a plane in a country that felt amazing, that's your Green Flag. One of my green flags is, I picture myself in my little cabin down by the stream dipping my toes in the nice fresh water. The other one I use is the amazing feeling I get when I get the "Look" from a dog while doing the Attentiveness training. That feeling always warms my heart, it fills me up.

This exercise is good to do when you are working, or about to work with your dog. Always work with them in *Green flag* mood, energy and emotion.

Lead work

There are three types of lead work - Your walk - the dog's walk - and the long lead walk.

Every walk should have both your walk and the dog's walk, - your walk for the connection and the brain work, and the dog's walk for the sniffing and toilet etc. Change it up on the percentage of each walk. One day you might do 30% your walk, the next walk might be 90% your walk, do not be predictable. The lead I use is 245cm long and a soft cotton mix.

Your walk:

On *your* walk, the dog must focus on you and your walk together. No sniffing or toilet, this comes when you are ready for them to have *their* walk.

Your walk is when the dog is walking beside you and focusing mainly on you. The opposite of this is when the dog is sniffing around and doing its own thing. It is very important that the dog gets a bit of both.

Let's concentrate on your walk, the human's walk. To start with, stand still. There must be some slack in the lead which means the clip is down so there no tension on the lead - there is a small smile in the lead. If the dog is on the left-hand side, you hold the lead in your left hand and then the excess lead is held in the right. The reason you must have the handle of the lead in your other hand is so that when there are dangers coming towards you, you can drop the left-hand lead which stops you from holding a tight lead when there is danger ahead. Remember the fight and flight reactions when you have that lead tight.

So, to start with, you stand with your dog beside you and get the focus from your dog. You need to have done the Attentiveness training first for this to work. No matter how long you have been walking your dog, whether it's been two weeks or twenty years you MUST get this focus first. The dog looks at you, you praise it, then you walk off. You do not say heel, you do not say come, you do not say the dog's name. When you've got a dog on a lead like that, your dog is to come with you. Once again this is a Behaviour way to walk a dog not an Obedience way. An obedience way would be to say - *come - heel* etc. The ONLY thing to say on a behavior walk is *good dog* or whatever its name is, every time the dog is shoulder to shoulder with you. It doesn't need to be looking at you but it needs to be focusing, even just slightly, on you. You say *good dog* and use a happy, pleased tone. You don't praise the whole walk, just enough to keep it engaged.

When your dog walks ahead of you, do not pull it or snap it with the lead. If you are walking with your dog on the left, you must have your left hand held tight to your body so you do not move that arm, maybe put your thumb through the loop of your trousers or in a pocket. It is very important that you do not snap your arm back. When your dog is in the wrong place it will reprimand itself by getting pulled on the lead because you have changed direction. The key to this is that as soon as your dog comes back, or looks at you, or looks like it is coming in the right direction, - you praise it. Don't growl if it is in the wrong place, you are only allowed to use a *praise* in this exercise, never a growl. If your dog is in the wrong place, you change direction, if your dog is in the right place, you praise it. It's that simple.

If you are having trouble getting your dog to focus on you, just move your leg, the one that is closest to the dog, until the dog starts looking at it, then praise. Remember if the dog is not doing this correctly it is because it does not understand, it is not because it is bad or naughty, it is because you are not showing it correctly, do the attentiveness training again.

Don't do this exercise fast because if you go zooming here and zooming there the dog won't know what to do. And don't be predictable, don't go around and around and around in the same direction in the same place. You must be unpredictable with this exercise. You might want to start doing this in your lounge, you go left, then you go right then you go backwards then you go forwards. Change direction to where you want to go because as soon as you take a step to where the dog wants to go, the dog is then in control of the walk. You must decide where you want to go and stick to your decision. Every time you step back towards the dog because the dog wants to go that way, you are losing points and you will lose the walk, it is no longer your walk. Once you get good at this exercise try doing some dancing steps, your dog at this stage should want to follow what your leg is doing, and make it fun.

Recap:

- Make sure you start at the start with your dog beside you
- Get the look - Praise
- The lead must have a smile and not be tight (Tight is fight)
- Only praise, never growl
- Don't snap with the lead, you must only use your body. Your hand must stay firmly on your body.
- Loads of love, lots of praise, lots of smiles - make it fun. Walking on your walk has got to be FUN

Remember this is important mental work for your dog and beautiful connection building.

The dogs walk

On this walk, they are able to sniff, pee and generally be a dog.

Your lead is about six feet long, you are holding the handle of the lead. The dog is still not allowed to pull on the lead. When the dog gets to the end of the lead you give it a little tug and as soon as there is a slackness in the lead you praise your dog. It can sniff, it can poop, it can mark, do whatever it wants, it is the dog's walk - but it is still never allowed to ever pull you on a lead. (Tight is fight). Still Loads of praise when the dog eases its pull on the lead, and remember, no growling. You might have to use the word "*Leave*" sometimes on this walk, that is good practice.

Long Lead work

This work is best used when your recall is not 100% or you are somewhere where you don't trust the environment. There could be protected birds or baby prey that need protecting.

For long lead work, get yourself a horse lunging lead, a pony lunging lead or a rope, but not cord because if it gets caught around your legs you will get massive rope burn, or it could cut the dog's leg. And don't use extender leads because all you are doing is encouraging your dog to pull on the lead. And they are also very thin which can hurt you and the dog. Equipment is very important here.

Distance control.

Until you have full voice control over your dog it should not be off lead. Can you call your dog off distractions? Have you got 100% recall? Can you stop your dog eating things on a trail with your word *Leave*? If the answer is no to any of these, then you need to have your dog on a long lead. This should be seven to fifteen metres long. I use a horse or pony lunging lead or soft rope. Practice how to roll up the lead before you leave the house or you will get yourself tangled up.

When you go between short or long lead, you do not need a command as your dog will know it has more lead now.

When your dog tangles you up on a walk

Place your legs a little bit apart so that you have a good strong stance for this because if you don't, when the dog tangles you up you will fall over. As your dog tangles you up, you tangle it up more until the dog lead is really tight around your legs. Then you stop, you don't say anything, you just stand there. Some dogs will stand there for ten seconds and then go 'oh shit this is not working anymore', and then untangle themselves. Now I have had dogs that have made me wait five or ten minutes in that position. I will still not untangle that dog. What happens is, they will pull even tighter and that's okay because what you are going to do is just stand there, look at them and laugh, this lets them know it isn't bothering you at all. If you are cross or frustrated when you do this they have got the result they wanted. When your dog finally starts to untangle itself, which I promise you it will do, you are going to say '*good dog*' let the lead go loose and walk out of it. If the dog attempts to tangle itself up again you do the same thing. I have never had a dog do it three times because it learns that 'that sh*t don't work no more'. So when your dog goes to tangle itself up, whether it is on your walk or its walk, you tangle up tighter. Do Not untangle your dog ever. Another thing they might do is they might not tangle you up but they might tangle themselves up. They will tangle themselves in amongst their legs and wait for you to lean down and untangle them. So what you do instead in this case is, you pull the lead a little bit higher and put your arm up, they will soon learn that if they tangle themselves up, you, as their slave, will Not untangle them anymore.

Recall

Do not expect your dog to understand the word '*Come*' just because you have said it. You need to set yourself up for success not failure. Often, I see people running after their dogs calling '*come here*'. These people are teaching their dog that '*Come Here*' means run fast away from me. If your dog has bad recall, it is because you do not have their respect or they do not understand what you are wanting. People often say, 'they just run away because they are naughty', no, no, no, they are not naughty, you just need to up your training with them.

Long lead work is the best and easiest way to train for recall. Each time your dog is walking or running towards you, call *Come* and the dog's name then praise. Each time they walk away, don't say anything. Do not say *Come* when you are tugging the lead, wait until they are happy and coming towards you. The word *Come* needs to be a happy experience everytime.

How to put the lead on without your dog jumping around

Do not get your dog excited by saying, 'walkies' or 'let's go for a walk' in an excited tone, that is just setting yourself up to fail. Get the lead out and when your dog gets over-excited stand up and pull the lead away from the dog. As the dog calms down, try putting the lead on. As soon as the jumping around starts again, pull back, never put the lead on when your dog is jumping around. This will take several goes but the dog will learn that when it jumps around, it does not get the lead on. Do not get too excited with the praise, just a nice quiet *'good'* is sufficient rather than a loud 'YES - GOOD DOG' as they will get over excited again. Don't forget, do not start your walk without doing the Attentiveness training first. Always start calm or do not go.

Lesson - Josie and Sammie

Sammie was a very busy huntaway, a New Zealand cattle dog, so it was important that she had a lot of exercise and mind work as she was bred to move cattle and sheep over distances. Josie had a beautiful park close to her home but Sammie kept on getting tangled around the trees, making the long lead work a challenge. I told Josie that Sammie was doing this intentionally and she needed to stop untangling her. I got a call a week later, Josie was frustrated, so I made a time to meet with her and we went for a walk together.

As expected, Sammie went and got herself tangled around a tree and she went around three times so it was a real tangle. I stopped Josie from walking up to untangle her, and still Sammie was holding her ground. She started crying, tapping into Josie's emotions. We both turned with our side to Sammie so we could just see her but not being obvious about it and we started laughing with each other. Sure enough Sammie untangled herself and came up to see what was so funny.

You may have noticed that when you are walking your dog it might stop, and start scratching its ear, scratching its neck or biting itself, that's because it is not getting its own way. So what often happens in this instance is, you stop and go 'oh it's alright,' and give it all that sympathy bs - stop it. This behavior is purely a distraction to get you to stop doing what you're doing. They are very clever, more points to the dog.

ASSESSMENT SHEET

Time to check in and see how you are going. No one will achieve a score of 5 in all or even many of these tasks. Perfection is Not the goal here. Do not expect a perfect dog the same way as you would not expect a perfect person, no one is perfect, we just want to strive to be better. This is a sheet to use as a progress sheet and a goal setting tool, don't be too hard on yourself. Be honest with how you feel you and your dog are doing at each stage.

Dog's Name: Age:

Breed: Today's Date:

How to rate your dog's progress:

ACHIEVEMENT LEVEL	SCORE
Absolutely Wonderful, no improvement required	5
Best efforts, just about there	4
Could have been better, understanding just no follow through	3
Did try, well ok needs to try harder	2
Effort was not really there	1
Forget it, epic fail. Come on human I do not understand	0

Dog's Training - score 1 to 5 for each action - with 5 being the highest score

ACTION   **SCORE**

Do I look at my human's face when there is trouble or I am afraid

How is my short lead work at home

How is my short lead walk out with distractions

How is my long lead work at home

How is my long lead walk out with distractions

Putting the lead on calmly

What am I like around my human's food

Is my barking a problem

My obedience commands. Sit- stay- wait

How is my mat and/or crate training going

Am I doing well when guests arrive

Recall at home

Recall out in public with distractions

Boundary work, keep out of the kitchen, don't go out of the gate

Respond to the word "Leave"

Dog reactive

People Reactive

My reaction to loud noises

Obsessive behavior

Separation Anxiety

Vet Check by my human

Vet check by the vet

Nail clipping

Date and Total Score

    Human Training Self Check - score 1 to 5 for each action - 5 being the highest score

ACTION	SCORE
Has my human done attentiveness training at least 3 times a day	
Has my human praised me enough	
Has my human taken me for a walk each day	
Has my human seen how my focus is casually around the home	
Has my human set up distraction training often enough	
How is my human's breathing and calm while training	
Is my human making more rules for me and sticking to them	
Is my human being consistent with my training	
Is my human using their emotions with their commands	
Total Score	

Vet check

How is your dog when you have to check something on their body?

Any vet, vet nurse, or groomer should be able to check your dog, and that is all parts of your dog's body. It doesn't matter if you got your dog as a puppy or as an older dog, it is so important that your dog can get a physical check over and be calm while it is happening.

The first step is - have a command - I call it *Vet Check* and I will check some part of my dog's body, maybe checking the teeth. The next step is getting your dog to look at you, praise, say *vet check* and with a smile look at your dog's teeth, then praise in a happy tone. This only lasts for a few moments, then a soft pat and walk away.

The next time you do this, try a different part of the body, maybe a foot, *vet check,* smile, pick up the leg and if the dog is happy, say *good dog*, stroke the leg and walk away. Stop the praise if there is any struggle and praise when they stop. If the dog struggles from the start, just hold that part of the body a little less. Do not pull away if the dog moves away, they will learn that if they struggle or move away, they win. This must not happen.

The words *Vet Check* must be fun and never a bad experience.

Things you must be able to do to your dog:

- Pick up their feet and check their pads and between their toes.
- Lift their tail and look at their bum
- Feel their tummy
- Check in their ears, get a tissue and clean their ears. I always smell the tissue to note if there is a bad smell. If there is, you must see your vet as it could be an infection or your dog could need a dog friendly ear cleaner.
- Wipe their eyes

To clip your dog's nails.

Often people have made the mistake of clipping too far or holding the dog's leg too tight. This has either caused mistrust or, they have felt anxious when they start because they are expecting the dog to struggle. If you *feel* a struggle, you will get a struggle. If your dog fights getting its nails clipped, each day you must pick up your dog's foot and with your fingernail touch their nail and say '*Clip*' smile and be happy about it. By doing this each day, they know that '*Clip*' is a fun word and they will not be hurt. After they feel safe with you doing that, use the clippers to touch their nail but do not clip their nail yet, wait until they relax when you are doing this and make sure YOU are relaxed and feel confident. You need to *fake your brave* here if you have to. The first time you clip their nails just do the very tip so you do not cut the quick and make them bleed.

Keep this simple, do not make a drama out of it, or over-react, as they will feel there is a problem. It is the same when you walk into your vet's office, you must *feel* happy about it, *fake your brave* so the dog knows that you have their back and they will be safe. Yes, the vet and clipping nails can be fun for them, if you make it fun.

Am I aggressive with my dog?

How much are you fighting with your dog?

There are several different ways in which we are too aggressive or rough with our dogs. It could be as simple as patting it too hard. Your dog could view hard patting as if it is being hit or bitten.

Whatever you do with your hands, that is the same as what a dog would do with their mouths. Therefore, if you are hitting, patting, slapping (not stroking,) your dog, you are, in effect, biting it. So stop it, stop it now. Many dogs will mouth and snap at people simply for this reason, you could be patting your dog too hard. Watch for their reactions, does their head lower when you pat - hit them? Do they lick their lips?, which could be an *Ouch* reaction. How would you like it if someone did that to you? Would you like someone to pat you like that? NO? So stop it, stop hitting your dogs. Your dog doesn't want to mouth or bite you, it is just reacting to what you are doing to it.

How aggressive are you with your dog? Are you doing any of these things?

- Patting your dog - slapping/hitting or stroking

- Pulling the collar

- Picking your dog up

- Pushing your dog down when it jumps up

- Rubbing their ears

- These actions can be viewed by your dog as aggressive.

How to hug and pat your dog

Learn to read your dog's 'stress signals'. These can be a quick turn of the head, rolling on to their back, lowering their head or they might freeze until the pat or hug is over, or jumping around waiting for it to stop, sometimes this looks like excitement. They could even go as far as growling and snapping at you. There are many signals but these are the most common. It is hard to accept that not all dogs or animals like tight hugs and often there are many places on an animal they do not like to be touched or petted. I am not saying do not pat or hug your dog, I am saying learn how to do it so that you both get the good feeling out of it.

I often see people pat or slap their dogs. Yes, some dogs like a harder pat on the lower back at the top of their tail but slapping them on the side of the body often hurts them. Yes, you can rough and tumble and play fight with your dog, that is different however, still make sure you don't hurt them, as you could get bitten.

What you do with your hands is the same as a dog using its mouth.

If you hit or slap your dog you are in effect 'biting' it, you are teaching it to bite you and other people. If you stroke your dog you are loving it, grooming it.

Don't pat your dog on the head but yes you can stroke it. Don't rub their ears hard because it hurts and you can easily break them. However, most dogs like rubbing *behind* the ears. The way you interact with your dog can make a huge difference to the relationship. Are you loving it or hurting it?

Meeting a dog for the first time:
The biggest mistake people make is shoving the back of your hand towards a dog's nose. Try doing that to a person and see how well that goes. Let a dog come to you. Take a step back and put your hand down by your side, if the dog wants a pat it will come to you. Never go towards them, the dog might not like you, or strangers in general. Do you like everyone you have ever met? No? well it is no different for a dog. That goes for other dogs too, not all dogs like each other, and that is ok.

How do I stop my dog from jumping up without pushing it down?

Simple, put your hands flat on your body and without looking at the dog or moving your feet, turn away so your dog gets no attention at all. Then, once it gets down, give a small quiet praise. Keep doing this until the dog understands that it gets no attention for this behavior.

Sometimes you might come across an extreme case where their humans have been pushing and fighting so hard with the dog that we need to take the second option. Once again put your hands flat on your body, take a deep breath, and walk gently into your dog, this will put it off balance and it has no choice but to drop to the ground, then give a small praise. If this is not working you are still doing it with a fight or aggressive energy not a calm energy. Take a breath, smile, and do it again until YOU learn to be calm and not fight your dog by using aggressive or frustrated emotions. If you are using your knee to push the dog down you are still fighting it, stop the fight.

To stop your dog from jumping up on other people, growl at the dog when it looks at that person *before* it jumps up, and praise as it looks away. You know what your dog is about to do so you must reprimand for the thought not the action otherwise you are teaching it that it must jump on people then get down. It is not up to the guest to deal with your dog. If your dog does not listen to you at this stage, you *must* have it on a lead so you do not fail.

Sympathy Causes Fear

Empathy is ok Sympathy is NOT

As I begin to write this chapter I am on the verge of tears, this is probably one of the most important chapters in this book so PLEASE take the time to read and understand what I am trying to tell you here. Let's get one thing clear - **Sympathy is bloody cruel** - please do NOT sympathize with your dog. I know you care about your dog and you might feel that you need to let it know how sad or afraid you are for it, but your dog does NOT need to hear it, feel it or see it - you are only loading it up with fear - and that's not very nice.

- My dog is scared of thunder
- My dog hates fireworks
- My dog barks when there is something new
- My dog hides when something happens that he/she doesn't understand

When things like this happen, people often give sympathy to their dog. Please don't do this. Giving sympathy when your dog is in fear is only compounding the fear that dog is experiencing. When you say things like 'oh it's okay it's not going to hurt you', and you give them sympathy or shut them away in another room, what you are actually saying to the dog is, this person, thing, or noise is a problem. So what's going to happen? Yep, the poor dog is going to become more fearful. If you tell your dog 'oh it's okay' when they are fearful, you are telling them it's okay to be afraid and that's not okay. Stop being a numpty and stop sympathizing with your dog.

When visitors arrive and the dog gets scared for example, if you don't react and just ignore the dog or tell it to go to its mat, or growl for the behavior, it is soon going to realize that these noises or people are not a problem.

I often see dogs who have become aggressive because of the fear generated by their humans being too sympathetic. Sympathy causes fear, then fear can cause aggression.

'What should I do?' you ask. Well, there are two options here.

Number One:

Whatever the situation is, make it fun. As soon as you hear thunder go 'woo hoo, yay, this is fun', play with your dog. When you know there are going to be loud noises like thunder, lightning, fireworks, noises from the building sites in your neighbourhood, slamming doors etc, get your dog on a lead and get ready to play with them outside or wherever the noise or problem is. Every time there is a problem, you need to make it exciting and fun. You will need to set up the situation in the beginning, otherwise you will be too late to praise and have fun in a real situation.

If you ignore the dog when there is thunder or loud noises etc, you are ignoring their fear, you are not dealing with it. This is called avoidance. Likewise, if you put them in their crate, their bed or their safe place, you are turning that safe space into a place associated with fear. That again is avoidance, not good. You can put the dog in the crate *before* the frightening thing, as you know that is their safe place, but not *during* the frightening thing.

Number Two: Growl and Praise

When your dog looks afraid of anything give it a little *growl* followed by a big praise - make it quick almost like one word, for example - *Arrrt-good dog*. Growl at them for the fear then make the praise big, give a big smile and heartfelt praise. The whole goal of giving a little growl is so that you can give them a big praise straight afterwards. Growl at them for the fear, praise for them looking at you for guidance.

The praise is so very important here as we do not want to make the fear worse, however it is important to growl at the dog for taking that nonsense on, they need to understand it is not their problem to take on. If their tail is hard under their tummy, please be careful and gentle as we do not work with a fearful dog. Do not cuddle or pat your dog when it is afraid, give it space.

Don't let your dog go and hide somewhere and quiver. As soon as you sympathize with it, you are telling your dog that the noise is going to hurt it - that it's going to die or be unsafe, that is cruel.

The best example I can give is; when an animal in the wild hurts itself, the rest of the pack will come up, give it sympathy, and then they will leave, indicating that it is too weak to be a part of the pack, so effectively, that animal is going to die. Therefore, when you sympathize with your dog, that is being quite cruel because you are telling it that it is going to die and or not be a part of the pack anymore.

So change your mind set with that, say instead, 'hey this noise is exciting, let's go and have some fun'.

Karen and Candy - the Border Collie

Karen drove up the driveway to the Pet Lodge and sat in her car for a few minutes. I went to see why she and her dog Candy were not getting out of the car. I could see Karen was visibly upset and Candy was shaking. Karen was saying to Candy 'I am sorry I have to drop you off at Jail'. I tried to explain to Karen that what she was doing was cruel and it was upsetting Candy. I told her, 'You need to come in here with a fun energy or the dog will be afraid of the place'. I then told her to drive back down the driveway and come back in with the fun feeling that Candy is going to 'Holiday Camp' and that she will have so much fun. Otherwise, I told her, 'please do Not come back, as the dog will be afraid of the place'.

Karen came back about half an hour later with a totally different energy. Candy was excited and I took her into the Lodge. Candy had so much fun on her two night 'holiday' it was wonderful. I even posted a video of her playing with all her new friends.

The next time Karen came to drop Candy off, she was doing the same thing she did last time, she was sitting in the car crying. And sure enough, Candy was shaking because Karen's emotions were frightening her. I walked up to the car and told her to GO. I said, 'you have been told not to frighten Candy as you drop her off'. Her comment was that she was not calling it jail anymore. I was so cross with her for doing this to her dog, especially when she now knew better. So she drove out the driveway. What I didn't expect was for her to come back. This time Candy was so excited as Karen opened the car door, she jumped out and ran towards the Lodge to see her new friends. I explained to Karen that if she repeated her tearful behavior again, she could not bring Candy back as I considered it cruel to wind her up and set her up for fear.

The next time Candy came for a 'holiday' she was jumping around in the car so excited to be here that she ran into the Lodge with no drama. I could hear Karen saying 'Holiday Camp' with a smile. When I came back out Karen was crying, she said 'I was faking it just for Candy'. I told her she had done well and now she could see the difference for herself.

It is so important to watch our emotions when we put our dogs into situations. If people are sad when they drop their dogs off, it tells the dog that the place is something to be afraid of and it takes the Lodge staff longer to settle them. This is why dogs are afraid of the vets and a bath/shower, if you make it fun, they will see it as a good place to be.

Don't be a numpty - stop giving your dog sympathy - it is <u>cruel</u>

Find My Brave

We all have things going on in our lives, it could be new or old trauma, grief, fear and often these are close to the surface in our everyday lives. This can affect how we train our dogs and the results we get.

Mindfulness - Breathing - Meditation - Calm - Focus on breathing with your dog

Dogs do not hold on to their old trauma. Often if you are holding on to your own trauma, then your dog will feel it as if you are giving them sympathy. This will cause them more fear and they will not understand. Dogs don't sit there and think about what happened to them in the past, although they can get triggered by past events. You will often see a dog flinch as you go to pat it on the head. Some people will say that the dog must have been hit. Not necessarily, sometimes it might have just got patted too hard or perhaps it is used to being grabbed by the collar too aggressively. If they have been starved and kicked, yes they can get past it but not when we give them sympathy all the time. Much like people, if they are continuously given attention or sympathy for their past traumas, they will keep feeding off it.

Fake brave, if not for you, do it for your dog. Most of us have had, or been through, some form of trauma, whether it be hurt, grief, loss, depression, the list goes on. Some people choose to stay living in these emotions and let it rule their lives, others work on them and try to move on and find things to be grateful for. What many people do when they are going through something, is that they forget that their dogs can *feel* them and *sense* their emotional pain. Holding your dog while you cry every day, what sort of life is that for your dog? Yes, it is understandable that it does happen sometimes, just don't make it a lifestyle choice. This is where you need to fake feeling brave, if not for you, then do it for your dog.

Being in a sad emotional state during training will only *fog* the energy required to give clear communication. Remove your sad emotions - Fake it till you make it.

I am the power - *feel* it

Breathing - try finding a breathing App and practice everyday

Faking feeling strong for your dog can help you and your dog so much

Use your good energy vibrations by using the Green flag and Red flag exercises or alternatively, the lock box.

Your internal lock box

This is an exercise that can help when trying to find your *brave* for your dog's sake.

Put your fear in a lock box, just for now, this is not about hiding your feelings and never dealing with them again. For this you need a picture of a lock box, it can be closed with a key or padlock. You know whatever is in the box is always going to be there but for now you choose to keep it locked away while you are working with your dog. Most people just need a picture in their heads, some people need a physical photo, others need a real safe or lock box as they are a tactile person that needs to touch it. Whatever you need to help with this process, use it.

Step one:

While practicing, do this on your own, not with your dog, as this will only confuse them. Picture the box and the key, mine is a stainless-steel box with a padlock. I can feel the key go into the cold padlock as I close it up, I can hear the snap of it closing and I know that fear and anxiety is locked in there and cannot get out while I am working with a dog. It used to take me a couple of minutes to put that shit in there, close the lid and lock it as I would get distracted by thinking about the shit that I was about to lock away. Now it takes about one to three seconds and damn it feels good to lock that shit away. You need to practice this; it is not easy to start with.

Step two:

Take a big strong breath and *feel your brave*, feel your strong powerful core, know you can be your dog's protector.

Be kind to yourself, be patient, self-punishment does not help your dog

We never want to sweep our 'shit' under the carpet or punish ourselves for thinking about bad stuff. Sometimes it can be useful, when we want to keep ourselves safe and to learn not to repeat old unhealthy behaviors. We have to accept that what has happened in the past has formed us the way we are now and the sooner we learn to find the things we like about ourselves, the better trainers we will become. Learning to be grateful is a good first step. 'I am grateful I have a dog in my life', this could be a nice start.

Working on myself has made the communication between myself and the dogs so much clearer and just beautiful. I can now use more calm than assertiveness to train, as I have more trust in myself.

Everything has a positive and a negative in life. How do we know what happiness is if we haven't felt sadness - or what hot is if we haven't experienced cold. Some people may try to go through life without the ups and downs, but why would you want to? Yes, we want to minimize the downs, the pain, the scary, but once we look at them and recognize them, we learn how not to hold them in our system, how not to carry that weight around. Yes, we can use it just for a second, then we can put it in the lockbox in the back of our mind. We are not meant to forget things like traumas that have happened in our lives, but neither are we designed to carry them in the front of our minds and in our bodies. Dogs live in the moment, that should be our goal, living in the moment, at least while we are working with our dogs.

This is why I love working with dogs. They can show us how to live in the moment and not hold on to the trauma they have been through. People are the ones that keep the dogs in their trauma. So many people get caught up in the *'my dog is a rescue* and that is why they are like this' scenario. I am really sick of people using trauma in order to be an asshole. Yes, I very much understand what it is like to have to work hard not to live in that shit. Lucky for me, when I have a dog around me, I know I have no choice but to let that stuff go, as my training would always fail or at least not be so strong. The dog would feel my trauma and then they would remember their own or just feel the unsafe energy that I was projecting. Make your dog feel safe, put that shit in the lock box while you are working with them, fake brave - just for now. You could always use the Red and Green flag exercises if you find that easier.

Energy

Dogs work off energy, a kind of inner vibration. I was sitting with a dog the other day and I looked at him and thought, he looks sad and the more I felt that, the more he looked uncomfortable and not his normal happy self. It then dawned on me, I was making him feel that way as I was thinking about something that was bothering me. So I changed the narrative, I closed my eyes and thought of something I was grateful for and sure enough when I opened my eyes and looked at the dog he was back to his normal self, head up body language more relaxed. Very often when I feel a dog's body before a lesson it is hard or rigid. At the end of the lesson the dog is a lot more relaxed, spongy even.

Deepen your connection

We can't be upbeat or positive all the time, as much as we'd like to be, life happens and it can be hard, so what then? When life becomes overwhelming you might like to try this exercise.

Sit on the floor. (If your dog is too jumpy and jumps on you, start by sitting on a chair). Look at the ground close to the dog, not their face or body at this stage.

Hold a picture in your head of the last time you watched your dog in a relaxed state. You need to hold this picture in your mind while doing this exercise.

Use your breath, breathe in through your nose and out through your mouth as slowly as you can. Start bringing your breath down into your tummy, hold at least one of your hands flat on your tummy and feel it expanding with the in breath and emptying when you breathe out. The only thing to think about here is your breath, then once you have that mastered you can focus on your dog's breathing and calm.

Once your dog starts to become calm, you can then very slowly move to the floor, still sitting upright. The calmer things get, the further down you can move. Once the dog is fully calm you can slowly and softly move your hand and place it on the dog. Each time the dog starts to move around, stop moving and breathe. It is all about the calm, gentle, safe feeling you share here. This exercise can take some time to master, depending on how your training is going and your dog's temperament.

An example of this is when I was living at a train-and-board home with a Jack Russell terrier. It took a week for me to get on the floor and totally relax enough for the dog to fall asleep. I have done it with a Great Dane, an hour after I met the dog. Do not expect too much too quickly though, it takes the time it takes.

Lesson: Jan and Simon the black Lab

Jan walked into my training room, she was living so much in her trauma that I could feel it was either recent or maybe even currently still happening. I asked her about the behavior problems she was having with Simon and she said he was 'out of control'. What I hear when people say that is, 'my dog is confused and I have no idea how to communicate with it'.

This dog was running around the room and being a right pain in the ass. I got him on a lead and did the Attentiveness training. He was such a beautiful calm dog and it only took about three minutes until he just laid down and relaxed. Jan said he had never been this calm in a strange place before.

I looked at Jan and said, 'I don't need to know what your trauma or pain is all about, however, I can feel it is serious and rather current. The energy this trauma is putting out there is confusing and hard for Simon to understand. He feels it as weakness and he cannot trust that you can protect him, so we need to teach you today how to *Find your Brave*.

We did the Green flag and Red flag exercises and then the breathing square exercise. I showed her how to put her sadness and fear in a lockbox - for now. I told Jan I didn't want to know what she was going through as I am not a therapist and it would only distract from the training, so we just concentrated on breathing and red and green flags for the time being.

This beautiful Lab did everything we asked of him and he was keen to do more. He had the most wonderful focus and just wanted to please. At the end of the lesson Jan did tell me her story. She was currently in a mentally abusive relationship and was trying to get away from it but was too afraid to leave him. I explained that every bit of fear that she was feeling towards her partner, she was also putting on to her dog. Her fear, her hate, her confusion, her sad, her feelings of failure, how could she be a pack leader in that state? She couldn't. She said, 'It's ok I will *Find my Brave*, just for Simon'. That's exactly what I needed to hear.

Jan got help with her situation and yes it did improve the relationship between her and Simon. She had no idea how much she had been putting on him and herself. When I saw her a few weeks later she looked so strong and as she said, 'I have never felt so free and brave in my life'.

Avoidance

Avoidance is avoiding teaching your dog what the actual problem is. It is taking a shortcut, and that never works long term. Let me give you an example:

A client came to pick up their dog from my Pet Lodge and I followed them out to the car to say goodbye. The dog started jumping around in the back of the car like a mad thing when I went to pat it so I pulled my hand away. The client told the dog to *sit*, which it didn't do, so she repeated the word sit over and over again. I asked her why she was saying that and she said, 'so you can pat her'. I just said, 'well no she's just not going to get a pat while she's being a numpty'. Then the dog jumped out of the car. What if it had been a busy road and got hit by another car. Avoidance is never going to teach that dog to stop jumping around in the car or jumping out of it. Not dealing with behavioral issues is avoidance and can put your dog in danger.

So what we need to do in this instance is to give a *growl* and as soon as it stops, you softly say *gooood dog* with a smile, give it praise. Keep doing this until the dog is calm. If this is not working, start closing the door, then when the dog stops, *Praise* again. Don't put up with any over excited or pushy behavior. Teach them that *calm* is the good behavior that we actually want. A dog is not a malicious creature, it is not going to jump around and be an idiot just to piss you off. The dog is jumping around like an idiot because it just doesn't understand what you want from it. People say to me, 'my dog is so naughty', my response is that it's not the dog's fault, it's the human's fault for not knowing what they are doing. People need to pull their head in and say 'ok how can we fix this issue without avoiding it or physically holding it back'. You don't know what you don't know, so let's teach you how to get the results you want.

I tell every client who comes to me for training sessions to stop using the word *SIT*. They will then realize just how many times they use the word *sit* and this will highlight the many ways they use *sit* as an avoidance. Try it and see for yourself. Stop using the word *sit* for one week.

When your dog starts barking, don't put it in its crate. That's avoidance and it is cruel because you are using its safe space as a punishment. You can put it in the crate when they have stopped barking and be happy with them as you put them in. We all need time out, damn I wish I could get sent to my room to rest.

Training is all about *growl* and *praise*. Let them know what is wrong and what is right. Wrong is uncomfortable, right is comfortable - growl, praise.

Sit - Stop - Cut it out - No don't do that - Pushing - Holding down - Sound familiar?

So often, people ask their dogs to sit when they are trying to put a lead on, or asking them to *wait* before getting out of the car. These are all using avoidance and obedience to deal with a behavior problem, stop avoiding the problem and deal with it.

Once again none of this will work if you have not mastered the Attentiveness training with a lot of praise. For this behavior training you must have your release word ready and rehearsed. This word must NOT be a common word like OK, as that can be dangerous as it is far too common and can be said at the wrong time or in the wrong context, instead, use a random word like, *Zip, Cross, Free, Pop*, something that is not often used in normal everyday conversation.

Dog jumping out of the car on its own

You do not want your dog jumping out of the car when you open the door. Open the door a little bit so they cannot get out, *growl* as they move forward, then *praise* when they stop, close the door a bit and start again. Do this again and again, yes and again, until you can open the door without them jumping out. Stand there with the door open so the dog understands they do Not have control of when they get out of the car. This is best done at home in a safe place first, as doing it at the park first time is setting yourself up to fail, you can Not afford to fail. Then use your release word to let them jump out.

My dog steals food from the bench

You must set up the situation, do not avoid it. Take a small piece of cheese or something else your dog would want to steal (not their own food), and put something like hot sauce, white pepper or some other not so nice thing on and around the tempting food and walk away. This will let your dog know it is not such a fun thing to do after it has told itself off by having nasty experiences with stealing things. I am always very strict with dogs, they should never be in the kitchen anyway, use your boundary work.

Lesson - Kathren and Tippy

A client phoned me up one day and said 'I need your help as I killed my last dog'. I was a little shocked so I asked her to explain.

She was dropping her children off at school and, as was her usual practice, she took her dog Spike along for the walk. As always, it was a nice catch up with the other parents. She was about to cross the road and told her dog to *sit* as she had always done. One of the other mothers called out 'we will see you tomorrow', Kathren called back in a loud voice '<u>OK</u> see you later', the dog took that as its release word and walked onto the road into an oncoming car and got hit, the dog later died at the vets.

The point here is, never use a common word as a release word, and do not make your dog *sit* and *stay* on the side of the road.

I had a lesson with Kathren, Tippy and the rest of the family. They were still very much holding on to what happened with Spike, their old dog. I suggested they have some fun by making up new commands so that sort of thing didn't happen again. We all had so much fun making up new commands. The new release word was now Toothpaste - why Toothpaste? Kathren said it was not a word her children would ever say, let alone on the side of the road.

Not my sort of training

There are many ways to train a dog, most of them good. However, like everything in life, there are some bad ways of doing things. The reason I am adding this to the book is these methods are still out there and they are doing a lot of damage, often to the extent of making dogs aggressive or overly fearful. Training with trust, respect, and good energy gets better long-term results.

Hitting your dog with a rolled-up newspaper, or something else in your hand, is still hitting your dog, why would you do that? This one might seem mild but it's dangerous all the same. Hitting your dog does not get respect, it teaches aggression or fear. The dog might not bite you, but they could bite someone else, and they will be fearful - this is just cruel.

Hitting or kicking your dog, seriously - do I really need to say anything here. Physical violence is a sign of weakness. So NO, please Just NO.

Alpha hold.

If you roll your dog on its back and hold it until it stops moving, that is an Alpha hold. It's a dramatic hold in a dog's world and can be very serious if the timing is not just right, so I do not suggest it.

The next thing after an Alpha hold is **kill**. It was a dog training method that was used for many years until the trainers realized that it was such a precise movement that if it was done wrong, a dog would become aggressive. So forcing a dog on to its back is best avoided. You can play - roll them over for a tummy rub, but always use a command like 'tummy rubs' so they know you are not threatening them.

Pinch or prong collars

These nasty things are banned in a lot of countries and so they should be. They have prongs like nails on a choke chain and it hurts, it is cruel. If any trainer uses these, please find a better trainer. These chains work on the premise that you can *bite* the dog to a high pain level so they best behave or you will bite them again. Some say it doesn't really hurt, so why does it stop the dog so fast then? Once again, inflicting pain on a dog is teaching it that pain is the correct way to communicate.

Electric collar

Like the prong collars, these collars are all about training with pain. You can do better by putting the work in. I know of dogs that have died from these things. As we know, dogs are very sensitive creatures and feel a high level of frequency, so saying 'this won't hurt my dog or affect my dog', Oh come on people, really?

Choke chains - check chains.

Yes, same thing. If used wrongly it is a choke chain, if used correctly it is a check chain used for sound not pain. It is a check chain if you use it up the right way, if upside down it will choke your dog. I am ok with you using a check chain, however, I haven't had to use one in over 20 years because I am now a better trainer than I was.

Extender leads - ban the damn things I say. These can be a very dangerous tool.

Hulti or gentle leader

The head halter goes over the nose and pulls the dog's spine out of place to stop them pulling. You would stop pulling too if you were in that much pain. These can do some serious damage to your dog and they normally fight it anyway.

Too many treats

Over treating when training. As you know I do not use food treats for behavior training unless it is required for aggression training. I am not saying it is a bad thing to use treats, I am saying it is a bad thing to use them all the time or to use them as a bribe, the dog will know the difference better than you. Dogs will often 'make' you get the treats out before they will do anything, that is if you have not followed the strict treat training way the trainer has shown you. Treat training is ok for obedience and tricks but not for behavior training.

Not being consistent

Today they can jump on your bed, tomorrow they can't. The recall word today is "come boy" tomorrow it is "get here". Keep things simple. I always suggest to clients to put a list somewhere so that everyone in the house can see it. It is important to be consistent with rules and words.

Punishing for good behavior

This one I see far too often. Examples of this are:

- Calling your dog and picking it up to bathe it, or trim its nails, or to yell at it for something it did an hour ago.
- Telling your dog to go to its crate or bed when you are angry. The crate/bed needs to be a safe, happy place.
- Getting your timing wrong for the *growl*, this sends the wrong message to the dog.
- Yelling or hitting your dog when it finally comes to you.

Making a training session too long

Lots of short training sessions are better than one or two long ones a day. Three to ten minutes is a lot better than thirty to forty minutes, which could be too much for your dog.

Scolding after the fact

You have seconds to *growl*, or the dog has no idea why it is being told off. If they are not still looking at the problem, you have missed a chance to reprimand. Rubbing a dog's nose in whatever it has done wrong, I am not going to even bother explaining why this is bad, come on people don't be a numpty, that is just nasty.

Crate and Mat training

Crate and/or Mat training is a must. If you are reading this book your dog is possibly displaying behavior problems so it is not feeling safe. A crate is a good thing to get from the puppy stage as it can help a lot with toilet training, relaxation time, and general safety. The crate is also an important tool for separation anxiety.

The crate and mat must **always** be a safe and pleasant place for your dog to be in. Never use the crate as a punishment or time out. Never yell "get to your bed" in a nasty tone. No one is Ever to pat or do anything to your dog while it is in its safe place, no pats, cuddles, or growling, absolutely Nothing. This is the dog's very own safe place. KEEP CHILDREN AWAY! No exceptions!!! It is good if the crate is covered, except for the door. The dog is a cave animal and often likes its safe dark place.

How to crate/mat train

Have your dog on a lead, take them to the crate/mat and in a nice fun tone say 'on your bed/crate/mat' or whatever you choose to call it. As the dog is on the bed *praise*, then as it goes to jump off, *growl* and repeat, comfortable vs uncomfortable. Give a nice smile and praise as your dog gives up and lays down. Do not make a big deal out of it as you need calm for this. Do not get overly excited about the win or your dog will mimic the excitement and jump out of the bed. Wait for a couple of minutes and call the dog off the bed, once again no over-excitement, just a small praise and walk away. Do this three to five times a day until your dog is happy to go to bed with your 'bed' command, then do it once a day just as a reminder until there is no hesitation.

When crate training a puppy, I suggest one to three hours at a time at different times and never the same amount of time, except at night. If your dog or puppy cries, Never go to the crate or even look at them as they will soon learn that crying in the crate will get your attention. Only ever look, or get your dog, when it is relaxed and quiet. You make your mind up from the start how long your dog stays in there, it is not up to them. Please make sure they have gone to the toilet before putting them in the crate so that is not the reason for their crying to get out. They must be quiet for at least two full minutes before letting them out. Do not make a big deal or even look at them when letting them out, just open the door and walk away, no big deal right. Wait for your puppy to relax before giving it your attention, otherwise it will always cry to be let out.

Who answers the door in your house?

When a dog does not trust that you can take care of who is coming into the home, it will take on the responsibility of the new people or problem itself. 'Maybe they just get really excited to see new people?' Really, are they? Often it is an overwhelming experience for the dog. They don't know if the person is friend or foe, they don't know what is going to happen with these visitors. It is not fair to let your dog answer the door. This is where it is important to do the mat or crate training. Set up the situation, don't wait for a stranger to come to the door and then try and control the situation. You will get better results if you set it up when you are ready, otherwise you will just be losing points and it will take longer to get the results you want.

Once the dog learns that they do not have to take care of people at home, this often reflects on how they respond when you are out at places away from the home. You need to be your dog's protector and only then can they become your protector.

Often, we have people who come to our home and these people do not like dogs, I know right I don't get this either. Anyway, for those special people, we need to respect their strange reactions, and also to teach your dog it is Never able to say hello to that person or those people. With good mat training this will be a simple task.

Often, after the dog has been on the mat for a time, they will lose interest in these people. This is becoming a lot more common for people running a business from their homes. It is not professional for a dog to greet a client or business associate.

Play

Play is a very important part of behavior because:

- It strengthens the bond between you and your dog
- It helps with communication
- It can decrease stress levels in both you and your dog
- It helps with mental stimulation
- It helps to build a stronger connection of understanding between you
- Let's face it, we get a dog to have fun, so let's make it fun

Make sure when you first start with any games, do it in short bursts so the dog does not get bored or overwhelmed.

Fetch

Make sure you teach your dog to bring the toy back. Start this exercise on a long lead, throw the toy and when they pick it up, get very excited. Call them, and as they are coming towards you, *praise* and be happy about it. If they drop it before they get to you, calm yourself and turn away from the dog. Do not go and pick up the toy as they will teach you to retrieve the toy for them. If the dog normally stops playing this after three or four times then only do it twice, always end on a win.

Hide their food.

As you know, I do not like food bowls, I feel a dog should hunt for all of their food. For this you can use scatter feeding or puzzle food toys. Google comes in handy, as there are so many wonderful ideas out there.

Name your dog's toys. Hold one toy in each hand and shake one. As they are looking at it say its name ie: 'blue ball', praise the dog for looking at it then shake the toy in the other hand and name that one, i.e. 'Dino', praise when the dog looks at it. After you have done this a few times, say the toy's name without moving and your dog should look at the named toy, if it doesn't you will have to practice a bit more.

You can name anywhere from three to fifty, yes fifty, toys depending on your dog. Put them in a pile and ask them to get the one you have asked for. When they bring it to you, play with them and the toy and have fun.

Hide a toy

Once the dog knows the names of two or more toys, make them wait, while you go and hide the toy. Then instruct them to 'go get (*toy's name*)'. Do not make this hard to start with, just put it close by or just around the corner. Get very excited with praise when they find it. Remember, your dog just wants to please you. Once they get good at finding the toy or toys, hide them in harder to find places.

Obedience

Obedience is also a great way for you to have fun and connect with your dog - *stay, wait, walk back*. It is great mind work and useful in everyday life. Once you have mastered the Attentiveness training, teaching them obedience training is usually easy.

Guide your dog to do what you want it to do. Remember, they do not know a word or command until you show them what you are expecting from them.

Tug - o war

This is great play with a rope toy. Sometimes you let them win and other times you can win. It is always good if you win the last game but if you can't, just walk away otherwise they will earn a point by winning

Put your toys away

Yes, this can be a fun game also. Anything can be fun if you put the excitement into it. As the dog has the toy in their mouth tell them to put the toy away. While you are holding on to one of the toys, walk to the basket and say '*away*', then say '*away*' again as you drop the toy into the basket. Give loads of praise when your dog drops the toy into the basket then go back and get the next one.

Agility and obstacle courses

This can be done in classes, groups, or just on your own at home.

Water games

A sprinkler, a paddling pool or just a simple hose can bring hours of fun.

Dancing with your dog

Dance around getting them to mirror your moves. Put your dog on lead and when you move your leg and your dog looks at it, *praise*. When it turns away, move, and when it looks towards you, *praise*. Your dog will start mirroring your movements, just like the 'your walk' lead work exercises.

Find the treat

Get three lids or cups, put a treat under one of them then move the lids or cups around. Whichever one the dog touches, lift it up. If it is the correct one they can have the treat, if it is the wrong one show them the correct one but do not give them the treat. Make this easy for them to start with, the more they get it right the more they will want to play.

Take your dog swimming

Maybe play fetch in the water. Do not do this for too long as you don't want to over exercise your dog.

Playing with a friend

If your dog is a social animal maybe it will have a friend it will want to visit with. If they are an introvert this might not be their thing.

This list can be as long as your imagination, happy playing.

Separation anxiety

Separation anxiety or boredom?

Fear or feeling unsafe in their own skin?

Feeling your separation emotions and mirroring them?

There can be several reasons for separation anxiety to occur. Your dog could be emotionally unable to cope on their own. Often they will not feel brave, even when you are at home, so when you leave the property, or you leave them somewhere else, their world falls apart. Making a dog feel brave within itself is the key here.

Do you play a part in their separation problems? Dogs will often mirror their human's emotions and energies. If you are sad when you leave your dog, it will also feel sad, and it will feel unsafe. That is why, when you leave them, you should *never* say goodbye or make a fuss, it is cruel.

Basically, *Separation anxiety* is: You have put your dog in the position of being the CEO of your household - and everything else in its path. It is not coping with the responsibility you have loaded on it. I liken it to a parent being tied in a chair and they are watching their two-year-old child walk out the door and onto the road. The parent will start panicking, raw horrible panic. This is the most awful panic you could feel in your life. So you are putting that panic on your dog when it is in charge of your life. Hence when some dogs go through intense anxiety like this, they will chew through walls, they can break down doors, they can destroy your house. The pack leadership is all upside down. The dog is living in absolute fear. Separation anxiety is one of the most destructive things the dog can go through. Please learn to be the pack leader, that is so important here.

Is the dog following you to the toilet, or from room to room? When people say, 'I can't even go to the toilet without my dog following me', then you are being an arse for letting that happen. This is destructive, it is cruel and it is heartbreaking.

So what do we do about it? We change the pack leadership around, this may not be easy, however it is achievable by using this system.

Transference with a lot of these behaviors is also a problem. If we are going through a lot of stuff ourselves and feeling very vulnerable, we are inadvertently passing this on to the dog.

Let me give you an example:

At the time of writing this we have a beautiful little dog at the Pet Lodge. She's been here heaps of times and never had any problems and she's never had separation anxiety. Last time she came in, and now again this time, when she is here, she is crying and barking and has massive separation anxiety. I asked the client what was happening in the family. They told me the pack leader of the family had a heart attack just before the last stay. Now this dog is not coping with that because the boss of the house, and the boss of this dog, is now weak and just about died. So of course, this time when she came into the Pet Lodge, she was crying and barking and freaking out. Everyone around this wee dog is feeling vulnerable and scared and experiencing all these emotions that the dog simply does not understand. There's no strength around this dog at the moment, it's all vulnerability and anxiety. So what this family needs to do is pull finger and give this dog back her boundaries, and her rules, and spend more structured time with her. Every adult (over 15 years of age) in the house should be working with this dog, then it wouldn't matter to the dog if one of them fell over or got sick.

The second time the dog came in a couple of weeks later, the uncle had died so there was more fear and unsure emotions around this dog's home.

So the other people in the house, apart from the one who is sick of course, need to stand up and make this dog feel safe. This could be as simple as doing the breathing exercises, *feeling your brave, faking your brave*, and sharing that energy with your dog. I do understand that grief is hard, and working with your dog is not in the forefront of your mind at this time, however, it can also be a helpful thing for you to do for yourself. Helping your dog often helps you.

Sometimes destructive behavior can be mistaken for boredom. Has your dog got enough mind work to do? It could be destroying things or barking at everything just because it has no job. Dogs do have a mind that needs to be occupied or they will find their own work to do, and it is not always the work that we want from them.

Boredom

Your dog needs a lot more mental stimulation. Just going for a walk and cuddles is not enough for a dog like this. Puzzle toys, focus work, scatter feeding, agility, scent work, there are many options out there. A dog is not meant to just sit around and be your cuddle toy when you feel like giving them some attention; they have a working brain and they need to use it. If you do not have time to work with your dog each day, you should not have a dog or animal in your life.

The more rules a dog has, the safer it feels

There are several steps to dealing with separation anxiety, there is no quick fix here. You will need to do a lot of work on changing your own habits for this process to work. It is about a six-week process and that is only if you stick to the Dog Logic NZ program and *change Your habits*.

The following steps can help you overcome Separation Anxiety.

As we know you Always start with Attentiveness training.

Step 1 Stop doing what your dog tells you to do, (stop losing points).

Step 2 You must crate or mat train your dog

Step 3 Set up situations like answering the door and lead walking and (gain points)

Step 4 Give your dog more thinking jobs to do

Step 5 Do not let your dog follow you around the house

Step 6 Never say hello or goodbye to your dog for at least ten to twenty minutes when you leave the house or when you come home. When you get up in the morning do Not say anything or look at your dog first thing.

Step 7 Don't pat your dog when it TELLS you to. (loosing points)
Step 8 Gain more points by doing the exercises in the first chapter.

The reason your dog has separation anxiety is because they are in charge, or your emotions and energies are telling them there is a problem!!!

Lesson - Janet and Steve with Brutis

I got called to a separation anxiety lesson. Janet and Steve told me they couldn't even go to the toilet or out to the letterbox without Brutis losing his shit. He would be barking, crying, jumping up at the door.

I got to the house and was greeted by Brutis, this stunning black German Shepherd. He was beautiful, and huge. He lunged himself at me and I turned so he could not connect with me. They had him on a tight lead but he was still lunging at me to let me know he was the boss around here. I asked them not to have him on a tight lead and to let him go as they were baiting him with me, causing this behavior.

If you have a tight lead, you are telling your dog there is a problem and they must fight or deal with the problem. That was their first mistake.

They dropped the lead. I did a slight turn with my hands on my body each time he lunged himself at me, and then he stopped. I praised him when he got down. I had told the couple to stand back, not to intervene and to just breathe. The whole energy was fear, he was going to hurt me, and everyone just had to calm down and shut up. All this chaos lasted about three minutes and they could not believe that he had stopped jumping at me after they did what I asked.

The problem is normally that they, like most people, will put their dogs in another room, so they are teaching Brutis that people are a problem. Keeping him on a short lead is telling him the guest is a problem. Yelling at him, that also tells him I am a problem. Grabbing at him and holding him back is teaching him to be aggressive to guests. As luck would have it, things had not yet come to aggression. With all the tools they were using so far, they were just teaching aggression, as the whole meeting people process was always met with fear, chaos and negative energy. This dog was in control of everything and they had let this happen by not understanding what they were doing.

As I say to my clients, it is not your fault, it's likely that you have been given so much wrong information or read several different dog training systems and mixed them all up.

Through this whole time of greeting me at the door, Janet and Steve kept trying to give Brutis treats. Obviously, that was not going to work, this dog was in full chaos mode. I told them I do not use treats at all for behavior problems and to please put them away.

When everything was finally calm, they showed me the back of the front door. It looked like a huge bear had attacked it. The door was a mess, it was an old solid wood door that was so far gone it was irreparable. When I commented 'Oh shit', they laughed and said that was not the worst door, that would be the bedroom door.

What they didn't tell me on the phone was that the reason they really called, is because not only were they no longer able to leave their house together, they weren't able to kiss, hug or do anything else together. They had resigned themselves to the fact that Brutis had to sleep in their bedroom or he would attack their bedroom door. There was a huge hole in the door. One day they tried to have an adult cuddle in bed and Brutis totally lost his shit. He ate a hole in the door big enough for him to get through and join them in the bed. They said they went shopping for a replacement door and the door salesperson was a client of mine and he suggested they call me before replacing the door.

Each time Janet and Steve had a kiss or a cuddle, Brutis would jump up between them, another way he was earning points, he was in control of everything, including their relationship.

So what did we do? You guessed it, we started with the Attentiveness training. We did a lot of lead work, made up a ton of rules, including not to jump on the bed unless invited, and then it was only for a cuddle then he must go to his own bed. They still wanted him in their bedroom and that is their rule so I was all good with that. He was, by invitation, able to join them on the couch but not the chairs. We did a lot of mat training and answering the door. After that, Brutis was so tired he just slept.

I spoke to Janet and Steve a week later and Brutis loved his demotion in the pack. He would sometimes forget, and all they had to do was growl and praise and he would relax again. And yes, the most important part was that the couple were able to have their adult cuddles without being 'told off' by their dog. Janet's comment was, 'thank you for saving our marriage'.

Feeding your dog

How and what you feed your dog has a lot to do with its behavior. Some people think that making your dog 'sit' and 'stay' for its food is a cool trick. To me this just doesn't make any sense. It might be an easy trick but it's totally pointless and not a nice thing to do to your dog. We are trying to make your dog *less* food aggressive or obsessive, not more. If you put a bowl of lollies in front of a child and tell them to *wait*, that is just cruel and pointless so why would you do it with a dog? Doing this often brings on food anxiety. Dogs will go into a panic over their food either by overeating or under-eating.

It is an obedience command that is very easy to achieve but consider that if you give your dog a command to eat, when it stays with someone else and they do not have that command, your dog will not eat freely. This is just cruel.

I do not believe you should feed your dog in a food bowl or from your hand, *ever*. So how do I feed them? Hunting is how. I have one biscuit that is readily available, normally in a treat ball. I have five different types of treat balls and puzzle toys. Then when I feed another type of bickie, I scatter feed or put it in a puzzle toy or a snuffle mat. You can make several types of fun feeding puzzles at home, Google is great for ideas. When I feed raw food, I make it up in frozen cubes and scatter them around in the grass. When I feed a whole raw egg, I toss it on the grass for the dog to play with. The first couple of times you do this, you might have to crack it for the dog to understand what it has to do. I do this once or twice a week.

I always make sure my dog has three different types of food, 1 raw - 1 large bickie - 1 kibble premium food. Many dogs have sensitive tummies because they have only eaten one type of food all their lives. Dogs thrive on a diet with variety. Keep your dog away from food colourings and avoid most canned food and dog roll because they are just junk food. I am not going to go into all the foods on what to eat and what not to eat, that is a whole book on its own and there are some very interesting reads about food. I would avoid the ones that the food companies write, I would take their information with a pinch of salt as they are just trying to sell you their food.

How much grass does your dog eat when it is out? Is it eating the top of the grass or the whole plant? Is it eating roots or bark? Is it eating dog or cat shit? If so, this is because your dog's diet is often lacking and it may need vegetables, berries, perhaps some oil, or several other things you can look into.

As with humans, if our diet is not right it can affect our behavior. You know yourself that if you eat crap food you will feel like crap, even some good foods might not make you feel so good. This can be the same for a dog. Too much wheat, rice, or potatoes, can be hard for some dogs to digest. Find what works for your dog. Often, canned dog food is mainly just water and fillers, you are better to use real pet food meat, like pet mince. Watch how many carrots you give them as these can have a lot of sugar in them, so if your dog is a high energy dog, carrots can make them worse. Food is such an important part of behavior.

Overweight dogs

Dogs will suffer many more health problems if they are overweight. You know you are being cruel by making your dog fat don't you! Food is NOT love. So how do we fix it? There are three different options here.

If your dog is really food obsessive, I suggest you go and purchase a very large bag of dog bickies and bucket feed your dog.

Bucket Feeding

Fill up a big bucket of food and let your dog eat as much as it likes of that one food. If your dog is a panic eater, not knowing where its next meal is coming from, the only way for your dog to get over this is to bucket feed it. The panic normally goes away after about 48 hours of eating too much and it will either be throwing up and/or shitting a lot. This will stop when your dog understands that the bucket will never be empty again. After about a week of this method of feeding, your dog will eat less when you feed it because it no longer has to panic about food. This is when you bring in the other one or two foods, but only in small amounts. Make them hunt for the food. As your dog is no longer panicking over its main food it will self-regulate and start losing weight. This can take two to five weeks, just be patient and don't give up. Do not take your dog for a run or let it play just after starting this process, or you run the risk of twisted gut.

If you do not want to do the bucket feeding method then I suggest you do not ever give your dog less food because if you starve your dog, it will hunt or always scavenge for food.

Try **Ice block Feeding**

Put some healthy food, maybe a bit of canned fish in oil, some vegetables, and a few of the dog's bickies, in a two-litre container and fill with water and freeze. I do this for one meal per day and the dog feels it has had a lot to eat as it has taken so long to get its food. With dogs that have been fed way too much and panic over their food I will often do this twice a day.

For a large dog you might want a bigger container, and for a small dog a smaller container. I had a small Chihuahua that was so fat it could hardly walk so I made all of its meals in muffin tins with water and it stopped scavenging for food and lost a great deal of weight without feeling like it was being starved. I also did this with a very large Black Labrador. He loves his fish and vege mix in his two litre containers.

The third option is to feed your dog the same amount using a **lower calorie diet**. Make sure you add things like celery and broccoli stalks for them to chew on so they do not feel like they are missing out. Please never feed less food as dogs eat to feel full.

Underweight dogs

Often this is caused by people who have been concerned with their dog's diet and have tried to give them something nicer, more tempting. The dog then expects you will change its food all the time. All they need to do is to wait it out for a meal or two and then their human, who has been well trained, will give them better and better treats.

Make sure you find a high fat and protein diet for this dog and have ONLY three different types of food. Their palate will get used to the food you pick for it. Only ever feed those three foods. A dog will Not starve itself to death. The only way to fix the damage you have done by spoiling your dog, is to stick to this strict new way of feeding. People often feed their dogs more than they need to. Dogs only have small tummies. Be strong here, food is not love.

I get many dogs with bad skin allergies and this will often cause behavior problems. This can be as simple as the dog not being able to tolerate beef, wheat, potatoes, food coloring, or some other crap that is in their food. With this skin condition and behavior combination, I suggest going back to 60% white meat and 40% veges for two to six weeks then look at adding one type of dry food. Sometimes a probiotic and fish oil can help ease the itchy skin. Keep your vet in the loop of what you are doing. Sometimes the best premium food might not be the right one for your dog, try another brand or a totally new way of feeding. When you make the 60% / 40% mix, make sure the veges are blended, the dog will get more goodness out of Raw blended veges. Nothing I feed my dogs is ever cooked, there are no stoves in the wild and that is how their digestive system works.

A lot of people are now feeding a 100% raw food diet. As much as I do like that, please make sure you do not only feed that one thing. You might want to add more veges one day, or if you don't like the bickies out there, make some of your own, change it up a little or add bones. Not many animals or people do well if they only ever eat one food their whole lives, they will be deficient in something over time.

My dogs do Not ever watch me eat anything. Each time your dog looks at you when you have food or a plate, you *growl* then *praise* when they look away. Keep doing this until they understand that when you are eating, they must Not ever look at you. When they look towards you putting food in your mouth, they should always look away then leave the room. Letting your dogs' watch you eat is cruel and makes for more food problems. Mat training is useful here. Treat training will only teach your dog that every bit of food you have belongs to them.

Making sure your dog has things to do, this helps with food obsession. That is why hunting for their food, and self-driven food games, are important.

ASSESSMENT SHEET

This is just to check in to see how you are going. No one will achieve a score of 5 in all or even many of these tasks. Perfection is Not the goal here. Do not expect a perfect dog the same way as you would not expect a perfect person, no one is perfect, we just want to strive to be better. This is a sheet to use as a progress sheet and a goal setting tool, don't be too hard on yourself. Be honest with how you feel you and your dog are doing at each stage.

Dog's Name: Age:

Breed: Today's Date:

How to rate your dog's progress:

ACHIEVEMENT LEVEL	SCORE
Absolutely Wonderful, no improvement required	5
Best efforts, just about there	4
Could have been better, understanding just no follow through	3
Did try, well ok needs to try harder	2
Effort was not really there	1
Forget it, epic fail. Come on human I do not understand	0

Dog's Training - score 1 to 5 for each action - with 5 being the highest score

ACTION	SCORE
Do I look at my human's face when there is trouble or I am afraid	
How is my short lead work at home	
How is my short lead walk out with distractions	
How is my long lead work at home	
How is my long lead walk out with distractions	
Putting the lead on calmly	
What am I like around my human's food	
Is my barking a problem	
My obedience commands. Sit- stay- wait	
How is my mat and/or crate training going	
Am I doing well when guests arrive	
Recall at home	
Recall out in public with distractions	
Boundary work, keep out of the kitchen, don't go out of the gate	
Respond to the word "Leave"	
Dog reactive	
People Reactive	
My reaction to loud noises	
Obsessive behavior	
Separation Anxiety	
Vet Check by my human	
Vet check by the vet	
Nail clipping	
Total Score	

Human Training Self Check - score 1 to 5 for each action - 5 being the highest score

ACTION	SCORE
Has my human done attentiveness training at least 3 times a day	
Has my human praised me enough	
Has my human taken me for a walk each day	
Has my human seen how my focus is casually around the home	
Has my human set up distraction training often enough	
How is my human's breathing and calm while training	
Is my human making more rules for me and sticking to them	
Is my human being consistent with my training	
Is my human using their emotions with their commands	
Total Score	

Aggression

There are several reasons for dog aggression, however they are often able to be overcome by using the same methods. People can get caught up with excuses such as, 'my dog is a rescue and that is why they are like this'. You need to get past that so you can help them move on from it.

Do the Attentiveness training first, this is ALWAYS step one. Your dog needs to trust that you can take care of this big overwhelming, scary, world for them.

'My dog doesn't look afraid when he is trying to kill or over-react to the person or dog', is another comment I often hear. Let me be clear, yes, they are afraid. Dogs do Not want to be aggressive, unless they are bred for that reason and have spent their early years being taught to be aggressive. Show me an aggressive person who, deep down, is not afraid. Aggression is built from fear. This is also why sympathy often causes aggression.

There are many levels of aggression, from mild to very serious, and there are many reasons for that aggression. The way to stop ALL aggressive behavior is the same, and that is, safety and security. So how do you get that? Yep, you go back to step one, Attentiveness training.

Another common comment I also hear now is, 'my dog was a covid lockdown dog so, we couldn't socialize them'. Stop making excuses for your dog and get them (and yourself) used to it now. Before you start with this exercise though, you must get your dog's trust first or you will simply make the situation worse. Please re read (Passive Dominance Vs Assertive Dominance). This is so important here, never use assertive dominance as that will increase the dog's aggression.

First and foremost - do the Attentiveness training

Then make sure you have programmed your dog to know that a quiet gentle calm pat or stroke means *'good dog'*. As you are showing your dog affection and saying *'good dog'* with calm and gentle energy, you are programming them to enjoy the *feeling* of the words *'good dog,* so you don't need to touch them while you are doing the Attentiveness training as the words are enough.

Don't go too loud or snap too hard and give them a very big smile when you praise. You are trying to make your dog feel safe and protected. You will really need to use your breathing here, feel your calm, make them feel safe. After your training, give them slow gentle strokes, not patting, slapping or hitting.

Aggression, Fear and Anxiety

These three things need to be defined.

Aggression is generally caused by anxiety and fear, therefore you have two different types of aggression - **fear aggression** and **dominant aggression**. If you have assertive or dominant aggression, that's really easy because that's just the bolshy dog that needs to be put in its place in a gentle loving way. If you deal with assertive aggression aggressively, this will make the dog more aggressive as they will do what you are teaching it to do and this is where passive dominance comes in. If you use assertive dominance for a truly aggressive dog, you will get bitten and you will probably deserve it. You do not use aggression to fix aggression. By the time I get an aggressive dog it has usually had electric collars and pinch collars and people 'Alpha hold' dominating them and people hitting them and all this sort of nonsense. They need love and understanding, not abuse. They need to know where they belong in the house, the pack. If they feel they have to take charge of everything, and they're not coping, that's what is creating that aggressive behavior.

Then there's **Fear aggression**. You deal with fear aggression the same way as you deal with assertive aggression. You do NOT deal with aggression by using aggression. When you use your hands to do things like pushing a dog down, smacking it, grabbing it by the collar or the scruff of the neck, what you are in effect doing, is you are 'biting' it because what you do with your hands, the dog reads that as what it would do with its mouth. In other words, you are teaching your dog to bite. Even when you pat your dog open-handedly or pat too hard on its side, your dog is reading that as biting.

'Why is my dog aggressive?' is a question I often get asked. The answer is - probably because you are doing something that your dog is interpreting as 'biting'. Try doing something that you've done to that dog with your hands, on another person. Now imagine doing the same thing with your mouth. That's exactly what we are doing.

People say they have kicked their dog, I tell them they have just used aggression. Of course the dog's gonna bite back, what do you expect? When I see aggressive dogs, I know it is because we are the ones who caused it, sometimes without knowing what we are doing. Dogs don't get all aggressive on their own.

How does a dog become aggressive?

A dog becomes aggressive because it's taught to use aggression toward aggression. It is either terrified by a situation you have put them in or you have over loved them in a way that makes them feel insecure. They feel they have to protect themselves against everything in the human world and it is far too much for them to cope with. A lot of aggression comes about from people who tell their dog, 'it's okay sweetie, you'll be okay, I'll make sure you're okay, you poor little thing'. That's just terrifying the hell out of them. Sympathy causes aggression, stop it.

Aggression is often very simple to overcome. Stop baiting your dog, stop terrifying it. Bring it back to where you are the leader, it is not in control, let it feel safe. You need to be your dog's protector. Your dog is not there to protect you, you must be there to protect your dog. Then in turn, it will protect you, but you must be the dog's protector first otherwise everything goes wrong.

If I see a 110-pound lady with a Rottweiler, she still has to protect that dog. That's hard for me to comprehend, hard for anybody to comprehend, and that's why we've got so many aggressive dogs. Here you have this little, petite lady with a big tough dog that's got four times her pull weight, and she needs to protect that dog so that it feels safe enough to do its job. If she doesn't have control, you've got an aggressive dog on your hands and you've got a world of problems. So why can a jockey control a horse? Well it is all about trust and leadership, no difference. When you get a jockey that is an ass towards the horse the jockey will often get hurt. Oh well they deserve it.

People ask me, 'Why is my small dog so aggressive?' Two reasons. Number one is because we pick the poor bloody things up all the time. Imagine for yourself what it would be like to have someone pick you up all the time. I'm sure you are going to get aggressive at some point or lash out at the person who keeps picking you up, often without warning.

If they tell me, 'Oh my dog is used to being picked up', well, I'm sorry but that comment is never going to wash with me. If you come up behind your dog and pick it up, it's going to get a fright. Stop doing it. Get their attention, ask their permission first. Have a command for when you are going to pick them up, this way they will get the warning, - 'up now' then in a gentle way touch their body and pick them up close to your body. Remember some dogs just do Not like to fly! Picking a dog up without warning or picking a dog up that does not like it, is an aggressive thing to do. Stop it, stop being cruel. Give them a choice to walk towards you or walk away. Do not pick your dog up all the time, I don't care what size it is, it's just not fair. That's why many small dogs are aggressive. They are nervous because they never know when they're gonna get scooped up. And people do literally scoop them up. Please pick it up with two hands and pull it in close to your body instead of flinging it around like it's a teddy bear. It's not a thing, it's a living creature, dogs are not built to fly.

Why don't cats like being picked up? Because people are shitty the way they pick them up. If you pick a cat up properly and do it the same way all its life, it won't mind being picked up. If you pick it up, like some people do, it's gonna hate it and most cats are smart enough to turn around and let you know about it in no uncertain terms, and good on them.

All those little dogs that are snappy and aggressive, we've made them that way. Carrying them in your purse is not good either. Once again, the answer to snappy little dogs is to do the Attentiveness training. You need to make your dog feel safe. Let it know that you've got its back, that it doesn't need to bite anything. Let them know you will deal with any scary things and situations that come along. Once your dog gets that message, the aggression dissipates, because it knows there is nothing to be afraid of anymore. You must have their back.

Aggression is one of my favorite lessons because the results are so overwhelmingly positive after a two-hour session. The dog completely flips over and goes, thank goodness I'm safe.

If someone tells me, 'my dog has been traumatized in the past and that's why they bite,' my answer is, 'leave that trauma in the past'. If you keep bringing it up every single day, of course it's going to be traumatized every single day. You're making it traumatized by holding that energy, it's always there in the background. Some people choose to stay in victim mode and keep their dog there with them. Stop it. Move forward. The result is beautiful, and oh so empowering. We can learn so much from our dogs, they like to live in the moment, not in the past.

Lesson - Family with Blue the blue healer

I drove up to this lovely old Villa and got out of the car. I walked up the beautiful green steps and at the top was one of those very large doors. This place was incredible. I was warned that this was an 'aggressive dog' lesson. I had asked them to please make sure that the dog was locked away so that we could have a talk before I met the dog.

This dog, Blue, was a three-year-old Blue Heeler. They are not normally known for full on Aggression, however, they can be very nippy because of what their job is, they're a heeler, they nip at cow's heels.

This was a family of mum, dad and two teenagers thirteen and sixteen years old. These children had not been able to have their friends over for the past two years. The family had put up with this dog's behavior for two years not knowing what to do. They'd had one trainer who had put an electric collar on the dog and all that did was make it worse. Then another trainer had worked solely with treats and all that did was make the dog more food aggressive. The family had to tie the dog up and put it outside when they were eating because the dog would lunge at them, demanding that they share their dinner or even a biscuit with him. A cup of tea wasn't even safe most of the time. The third trainer just walked out when they saw how aggressive the dog was and said there was no hope and that it needed to be put to sleep. This is when they asked their vet and the vet said, 'if Maree can't fix this then we will put the dog to rest'.

I knocked and a lady came to the door. As she opened the door, all I could see was this dog running towards me so I grabbed the door and closed it. The dog was running so fast that it hit the door with a loud thump. I yelled at her through the door and said 'put the dog away'. I was a little bit cross as this is what I'd already asked them to do. I could hear people scuffling around and the dog being put away. The lady opened the door again, she was extremely embarrassed. She said, 'I did put it away but it ripped out the chain when it heard somebody knock at the door'.

I could hear this dog out the back, growling and barking aggressively. They showed me through the window how the dog was behaving. Everybody was so distraught about what had just happened. They were on the last warning from the council, the dog already had a *dangerous dog* file on it and I was this dog's last hope.

I asked them what other behaviors were going on because when you've got aggression you've got other things as well, such as:

- stealing food

- jumping up and lunging at people
- having no boundaries
- barking when it wants its dinner
- pulling on the lead
- barking in the car - and this wasn't even the full list.

When you have aggression, you have a lot of other problems as well and that's because the dog has got no boundaries, it doesn't feel safe, and all these other behaviors around it prove that. The family were unable to take this dog for a walk when there were any other dogs or people around because the dog just didn't cope. In fact, it hadn't been off lead or walked in public for two years, this was a three-year-old dog. The dog was living in fear and nobody could see the fearful side, they just saw the aggression.

I sat down with the family and explained what we were going to do. I explained the Attentiveness training and I explained what was going wrong with the pack. These people needed to understand that they just needed to make Blue feel safe and protected in his own home again and then, when he felt brave at home and protected at home, they would be able to go for a walk.

This was one of the most aggressive dogs that I've come across in my career. It had bitten three people and the only reason it hadn't bitten more was because they'd kept it away from people. I was rather excited at this time because I could see behind all that aggression and after talking to the humans, I could hear how beautiful and loving and gentle this dog could be when not under pressure. They showed me photos of the dog cuddling up to them on the couch, outside playing softball, it was just when other people or other things became involved that the dog did not cope. Why didn't it cope? because it didn't have a protector, it was the pack leader and it was crap at it.

I stayed inside and through the glass door I instructed the family on how to do the Attentiveness training. Normally I wouldn't work with the teenagers, just Mum and Dad but in this case this dog needed a massively huge demotion within the pack. So once all four people had successfully done the Attentiveness training, I opened the door. I asked everybody to stop and breathe, because the tension, as soon as I opened the door, made the dog tense up. I shut the door and waited until everybody was breathing and calm and then I started to open the door again. When the dog looked at me, I told the mother to growl then praise as soon as the dog looked back at her. This took about two minutes and I was standing there with the door open the whole time. Everybody was in shock. I then asked the mother, because she was the one that got the better response from the dog, to walk past me into the house so we could sit down at the table and talk about how they needed to change their habits within the house.

We set up the 'Answer the door' exercise a few times until Blue no longer had any interest in the door and just went to his safe place. They had asked a friend to help with this exercise so I asked them to invite that friend over now. When asked, most of their friends had said, no they would not come over, as they were all afraid the dog would get out and bite them.

The family and I sat in the lounge and the friend knocked on the door. Blue was sent to the mat, his safe place. He was so tired after all the training he just went to his mat laid down and went to sleep. The 'stranger,' who was too afraid to come into the house before, was invited to come in and sit down on the couch. We'd also done couch work with Blue so he was no longer allowed on the furniture without an invitation. We were all sitting there and the mother started to cry, they couldn't believe the difference in just two hours. Quite simply, nobody understood this dog, nobody had gotten to the root of what was going on with his dog. Blue was amazing and sweet and gentle and he had been pushed into fear because his people didn't understand how to speak dog.

Blue now had a whole list of new rules and jobs. They were looking forward to doing agility training with him and all the other mind work exercises we discussed. Now this dog had jobs to do. Aggression was not one of them and over protecting the family was also not one of them.

These people kept in touch with me every week and told me how well Blue was doing. Six weeks later they had a barbecue at their place with ten different people. They said it was beautiful. Blue socialized, he didn't jump up on anybody and he went to bed when he felt overwhelmed because the strict rule of course was that nobody was allowed to touch him when he was in his crate or on his bed. This dog was not gonna die today.

Reactive dogs

Click into your human and they will keep you safe. The human will deal with any problems so the dog doesn't have to.

A reactive dog is a reactive dog no matter what it reacts to. It can all be dealt with in the same way. If a dog is reactive, it is generally scared of something or trying to over-protect something or someone. The dog, if it is in the right place in the pack, has no need to do that. It needs to look at you and go - 'well should I deal with this or should I go and bite it'. One look from you should say - 'no leave it alone'. Same as when another dog comes along. Your dog feels like it has got to go and protect you or deal with the other dog, as it knows you won't. If it feels like this, then you are not doing your job right. You need to be your dog's protector, not your dog being made to feel it is your protector, because that is just not right. And what I mean by that is, your dog will protect you if you protect it. It will not understand what it needs to protect if you are not the pack leader. It will feel like it has to protect *everything*. When there is another dog coming towards you and your dog is unsure about it, it will go into automatic over-protection mode and it shouldn't have the stress of having to do that. If it does, then that is your fault, not the dog's, and yes we can stop it.

We fix this by doing the Attentiveness training and the word *Leave,* and by putting more distractions in the Attentiveness training. Make sure you do the initial training somewhere safe first, like in the home, where someone might accidentally drop a piece of sausage or cheese or anything they might like. They are never allowed these things. You can't accidentally drop the cheese then give it to the dog afterwards. That's like saying 'oh you can't bite the child now but guess what, you can bite it in five minutes time when I hand it to you'. That's a big NO. It is not appropriate to ever give the dog any of the things you use as distractions.

After you have done some initial training at home and you are achieving good results, perhaps go to somewhere like a big park area where there are no other dogs around, nothing threatening coming towards you. Growing trust is important here. Until you get the respect and the trust from your dog, avoid places that cause your dog to react. A reactive dog does not trust you to take care of it. Some people will bring up a dog's history as an excuse. My response to that is - 'it's history, it is not current. If you stop living in the past, so will they. You can teach your dog not to be reactive'.

Breathing and calm is so important here. Practice, practice, practice your breathing exercises and also practice your breathing exercises with your dog. Learn how to breathe. If you have trouble learning how to breathe, try downloading a breathing exercise on an App or try a yoga breathing exercise. Put your dog on a lead and do that at least two to five times a day until you learn how to turn on your calm and breathing automatically. So when you see a dog that is two hundred meters away, you switch on that calm and do the breathing. What automatically happens when you have a reactive dog is that your heart rate goes up, your breathing quickens and you tighten your hold on the lead. You do all the opposite things to what you should be doing. You need to stop doing that. You need to use your calm, you need to use your breath, you need to use your *I am the power, I can help you here*, not 'oh my God we're gonna be scared and we're gonna get bitten and we're gonna get attacked'. That is not the way to keep your dog from being reactive. It could get your dog killed and get you hurt. This is unacceptable, you really need to use your breathing and your calm and tell your dog, 'well actually mate I've got your back, I don't need you to have mine here, I've got this'. Then you can keep both of you safe.

Always put yourself between you and another dog in this situation. Letting your dog go out in front and allowing it to lunge at other dogs is not acceptable. If your dog is on a lead and the other dog is free, you MUST hold your dog's long lead and only hold the handle. Your dog has two options, fight and flight and it is up to you what one they use. We all know these fight or flight signals; they are the same for all species. If you've got your dog on a tight lead, it has no option but to fight, and you are causing that by restricting its flight option.

When you are training your reactive dog, find safe places to work in first, take baby steps, don't set yourself up for failure. Each time you fail it is a huge setback for a reactive dog. You are better to do the Attentiveness training for a week or even four weeks, depending on the severity of the behavior, and do this at home not out where you are setting yourself up to fail.

Is your dog:

- Dog reactive
- Bird reactive
- Children reactive
- Food reactive
- Reactive to something else, anything else

The tools to overcoming these problems are simple. Do not over complicate this system. If you are aggressive here, the dog will also be aggressive. Breathe and be calm.

The word Leave

For training purposes, I use things like food/cheese, a soft toy they are never able to have. Throw something close to you on the floor, tell them to *leave* when they look at it, snap the lead as you say the word *Leave,* to make sure they do Not ever have it. *Praise* when they look at you, use *Leeeeeve* in a deep guttural tone when they look at the distraction. Do that a few times until they no longer think it is a good idea to look at whatever the distraction is. Make sure you do this exercise on the lead first so you NEVER fail when using the word *leave*.

Don't forget the *praise*, they will not work for you if they don't get paid, *praise* is payment.

Lesson: - Kirsty and Alfie - Dotterel training

Alfie was a foxy, a wee hunter, and he loved to chase birds on the beach. We'd had a one-on -one lesson about six weeks earlier and Kirsty phoned me to say she now wanted to tackle Alfie's 'birds on the beach' issue. As Alfie had so many other problems in and around the home, this was not something on her priority list when we met for the first lesson.

It was soon going to be the season where a local bird, the Dotterel, was going to hatch and as they can't fly for several weeks, they are just running around on the beach. As Alfie was such an avid hunter, Kirsty was naturally concerned. She lives close to the beach and didn't really want to stop taking Alfie to the beach during that breeding time. She had done the six weeks of boundary work with Alfie using the word *leave*, but he still wanted to chase all the birds.

So now it was time to let Alfie hunt and chase on command. Kirsty decided on the word 'Rabbit' as his chase word. You must master the *leave* word first though. As soon as the dog looks at the thing it wants to chase, you say *leave*, before he starts chasing it. Reprimand for the thought, not the action. So I told Kirsty to throw his ball and say 'Rabbit'.

Alfie was allowed to chase rabbits and when he found one, Kirsty would use the word/command 'rabbit'. So they walked around their farm and when Alfie looked at the rabbit Kirsty, in an excited tone, said 'rabbit' as Alfie was running - *good boy*. As we had previously done the boundary work, he would stop at the fence so Kirsty would yell *Leave* and he would stop.

After this was mastered Kirsty went to the beach with Alfie on a long lead. They were on the hunt for a Dottrel, the bird Alfie was NOT to hunt or chase. They found one in the distance and Kirsty pulled on the lead with a very serious *leave - good boy*. She only needed to do it a couple of times because when she said *leave* Alfie knew she meant it. They then found some sea gulls and Kirsty said *Rabbit,* and off he went chasing them down the beach. Yes, you can teach your dog to hunt one breed of bird and leave another.

Lesson - Jan and Pippa - Dog reactive aggression

Pippa was a very cute little Poodle cross Spaniel. We see a lot of these sorts of crosses now. Many puppy farmers call them 'designer breeds' and give them a new name like 'Cavadoodle' so they can charge several hundred or even thousands of dollars to make more money. It is a very sad new trend as, with many crosses, they often breed for the look and not the temperament. Yes, there are a few really good breeders that still do it well, it is just sad that the backyard breeders and puppy farmers are messing it up. The sooner dog breeding has to be licensed the better.

Pippa was from a puppy farm and at five months old the farmer decided they were not going to breed from her. They told Jan she was not the 'look' they were going for. I suspect they simply could not handle her so they passed the problem on to someone else, someone who had Never had a dog before. Yes, Pippa was Jan's first ever dog.

By the time Jan called me she was a mess. She hadn't taken Pippa for a walk in weeks as she was too afraid to leave her property with her. Pippa just wanted to attack every dog she saw. Jan had paid over three thousand dollars for an out-of-control cross breed dog, that's just criminal. The breeder said they were a first cross but had no papers to show that, unless Jan wanted to pay another thousand dollars for a copy. Just another lie from the breeder and unfortunately this is very common.

Pippa was now a year old and very dog aggressive. As with most aggression, there was so much fear in this dog it was heartbreaking. Because Jan had never had a dog in her life before, this lesson needed to be broken down into two sessions. First and foremost we had to get the basics sorted. We had to change her feeding, her lead was too short, she had no bed of her own so she had no safe space to go to in the house. And then of course the Attentiveness training had to be mastered.

Jan was very much stuck on, the 'Rescue' syndrome and the 'I am not strong enough' fears. We spent a lot of time working on her Green flags and deciding what her Red flags would be and then working on how to put them aside and focus on the Green flags. We spent a lot of time on Jan's breathing and calm. There was no way any of this would work without her feeling brave for Pippa. I told her that it would take three to ten days before they would be ready to go for a walk outside her property.

Do not go out the gate until you are ready or you will fail, you cannot afford to fail with a dog as aggressive as this.

Four weeks later I got a video from Jan of her and Pippa walking down the street. Pippa kept looking up at Jan for safety and guidance. Jan wanted to show me how they set up the situation for a dog to pass on the other side of the street and Pippa looked at Jan for safety. Her question was, 'do you think we are ready to go further than one block from my house? I was so very excited and proud of all the hard work she had put in and Pippa looked so different, her whole body was relaxed and bouncy, it was beautiful. Jan sent me videos of her and Pippa three months after that, with Pippa at the local Agility club having fun with the jumps and being around all the other dogs.

This dog will always have a level of fear as that is part of its breeding, but like most of us we can learn to work with our anxiety, especially when we have someone who feels safe beside us. This is no different for dogs and humans.

Barking

When training, using the Dog Logic NZ system, you must do the Attentiveness training first. Without that, none of the other things will work. You must have trust, and the respect from your dog before you do anything else. Your dog must understand and know that your growl is serious and that you're not just playing games, that is the only way they feel protected. You need to get your dog to look at you and then praise them. Remember, don't physically pat them while you're doing the Attentiveness training as you can't praise physically when you are at a distance.

With barking, you must always set up the situation. You can't tell your dog off after it has started barking because you're then telling it that it's allowed to bark but then it must stop. Also, what you are doing is barking with your dog by yelling at it, telling it to bark more, bark louder. So the only way to do this successfully is to set up the training situation.

If your dog barks at people walking past your gate, you need to set somebody up to walk past your gate and as soon as your dog looks at that person, you do a small growl and then a praise when they look away.

If the dog is barking at somebody knocking at the door, same thing. You get somebody to knock on the door and get ready to reprimand the dog for the thought and not the action. Dogs are simple creatures; they are thinking about what they are looking at. If you wait until they bark, you are teaching them to bark, then stop.

Mat training is important for knock-on-the-door work and so is boundary work. You need to let your dog know where it should be when there is someone at the door and NEVER allow it to greet the people. It is important to understand that a quiet whimper or sound is the build up to the bark, so stop it right there. I have a zero tolerance for a whimper or a cry.

Teach your dog to stop barking by making it bark

This is another useful tool to stop your dog barking. Get a squeaky toy and hold it out of reach and get your dog excited. Never let your dog have this toy - ever. When your dog starts to bark at it, give the barking command as it is barking. I use *speak - good dog, Speak good dog*. When the dog stops barking you say *finish*. Do this several times over a week and your dog will learn to bark on command and finish when it is told to. I also like to use a small hand command, so once the dog is good at this exercise all you will need is the hand command.

Lesson - Excessive Barking

I got called to a case where the Council had given these people six months of warnings. Just about every neighbour had written a letter to say, 'shut your dog up, we've had enough'. This dog was just barking all the time. He was a German Shorthaired Pointer x Huntaway, a NZ bred dog that is bred to bark and chase animals. Here you have a cross of two working dogs, and it is a stay-at-home dog without a job.

I drive up to this incredible place. It was two-storied and they had this wraparound deck, the house was amazing. As I head up the driveway, all I could hear was this dog barking. It was loud, very loud.

The dog's human let me in and shows me the letters from all the neighbours, she's a mess. She says, 'they're going to kill my dog. Council is going to kill my dog. I don't have a choice. I understand the problem but I don't know what to do about it, we need help. We have tried other trainers and all they want us to do is give treats to the dog when it is not barking. The council told us we have to put an electric collar on our dog. We tried that and all it does is scream, so we put it on a lower setting and it doesn't work. He started chewing his feet and the tops of his feet have no hair from the stress.'

These people, just like most of my clients, are the most beautiful, loving, caring, gentle souls, and that's the majority of the problem. They treat their dogs like their babies. They're not a baby, they are a dog. We over-baby and humanise them, which frightens the living crap out of them and they're scared. They're barking, they're screaming, and they can't stop because they're living with so much panic and fear, or too much pressure on them to do a job they are not good at. How are they meant to understand the difference between a good person walking down the street, and one who is going to hurt their humans?

Now this dog was pretty thin. The reason it was thin was because it had so much pent-up anxiety, it was wound up. It had to take care of every neighbour and every bird and every car and everyone who walked down the street and oh my god, those bicycles! You could see the panic in this dog. It was devastating. It broke my heart. The dog wouldn't shut up. I was trying to have a conversation with this lady and it wouldn't shut up. So, I did the Attentiveness training. It took about ten minutes until the dog looked at me and took the deepest breath that a dog can take, then it just lay down beside me and I got on with the lesson.

The lady was like, 'what on earth did you just do to my dog?'

My answer - 'I gave it permission to be a dog. I gave it permission to let go. And I told it that I had its back. I wouldn't let anyone hurt anything here, and the dog knew that, and now it didn't have to be on guard. That's what Attentiveness training is all about.'

This dog is now lying at my feet, I drop the lead. The dog is fine, it's not going anywhere, it doesn't have to go anywhere. It's got someone it feels safe with, someone it doesn't have to protect, it now has a protector. We have to learn that we need to be the dog's protector and not the other way around, then the dog will protect us when we need it, big or small.

We hadn't even started the lesson and this poor woman had tears streaming down her face and asked, 'how can I do that?' I spent the next two hours teaching her how to do what I had just done. It sounds easy, you growl and you praise and you get the focus and you give it all this love. And yes, it is that easy. That's what this whole book is designed to do, to teach you what I do, and that is: *'get the dog to look at you, praise or growl, then praise'*. This will generate Trust and Respect. But, if you don't do it in the right order, if you don't get the 'recipe' right, this is where things can go wrong. If you don't put the ingredients in at the right time, nothing will work.

We spent those two hours putting a lot of rules and boundaries on that dog. It had a lot of jobs now. It wasn't allowed on the red carpet in the living room. It was no longer allowed in the kitchen. It was no longer allowed in bedroom number three, but it was allowed in bedroom number two. We also started naming its toys. 'I want you to go get Blue Bear. I want you to get Dinosaur'. The dog was smart and he'd had nothing to do, he was bored shitless. I taught him all these games and it was absolutely beautiful. It now had to hunt for all of its food and we changed its diet.

You have to work out why your dog is barking in order to stop it. This woman sent me a message about a week later – the dog didn't bark anymore; it didn't need to. Yes, it took her being on to it and doing the homework, but now the dog knows what is expected and what is not. It now feels protected.

Lesson - Lifestyle block barking - big family

I drove up this very long driveway only to be greeted by three very big dogs, one was a big German Shepherd, the other two were Rottie Retriever crosses. The barking was huge, loud and intrusive. If I didn't know about dogs' body language, I would have been too afraid to get out of the car.

This lady had phoned me and said, 'I've got a little bit of a barking problem, can you come and help me please, I've got three big dogs.' I actually had no idea what I was coming into other than 'a little bit of a barking problem'. I sat in the car for a minute to watch what was going to happen, to see what was going on, and to see if they stopped. All that happened is that the dogs got worse. I got out of the car and walked up towards the house. One of the dogs jumped on me, another of the dogs pushed me and as I got to the lady I had a big smile on my face. The shocked expression on her face was beautiful. I said, 'this lesson is going to go so well'.

We sat down for a while and went through their wish list and whinge list, which I do with every client. I ask them, 'what behaviors do you want from your dog, what do you not want from your dog?' Obviously her main one was, 'we want to stop the barking' and I said yes, but there is more to it than that because if they are barking, there's a reason for it. We need to find that reason so that your dogs no longer have the job of barking at everything. They are bored and they think that they have to bark and chase everybody off the section. They think that's their job, so we have to reset and let them know what we do want from them'.

So naturally we started with the Attentiveness training and then we did short lead work. The focus from these dogs was amazing. The lady had done a lot of the foundation work because she had done obedience and agility with one of them. It was incredible the amount of time this woman had put into her dogs. She'd been working with them for a couple of years, and this whole time, I had only been there half an hour, not once had her dogs looked at her, none of them looked at her face. They all had their backs to her, they were guarding, they were taking on the responsibility of taking care of her. Even though she thought that was wonderful, it's not a safe thing to do. If your dog does not understand that you've got its back, it will have yours, and it has no idea what is expected of it.

After the Attentiveness training and the short lead work I said, 'now we need to set up a situation'. We made a place that we wanted the dogs to go to when people arrived, and that was their safe place. They no longer had the responsibility of chasing away the people that arrived. We set up something small at first. I hid around the corner and came walking out. Only one of the dogs barked and the other two just looked at her for permission. She growled at the barking one then gave a big praise for all of them. I banged on the wall; these are things that would normally set them off. They looked at where I hit the wall and she growled at them and praised straight away. The dogs settled and I could no longer get them to react.

Now the big one. They were a nightmare when people arrived in their cars so this was going to take some serious setting up. The power company, the couriers, no-one would come up to the house. Even some of their friends would no longer visit. They had two teenage boys so we got the whole family involved. We filled up three buckets of water balloons and told three people to hide so the dogs couldn't see them. I then drove off down the road. They had strict instructions to not let the dogs see who threw the water balloons. They were to try and aim beside the dogs, not at them (mind you a water balloon would not hurt them, it would just send the SNAP message). The point of this session is that each time they bark, a water balloon comes from nowhere and it is uncomfortable for them. I drove up the driveway and yes, they all started barking, then the water balloons started and yes, the dogs stopped barking. When the human came out, she praised the dogs and sent them to the welcome spot that we had trained them to go to earlier. We did this three more times and the dogs learnt what was expected of them. When someone arrived, they went to the safe spot. These people didn't want dogs running out to people, they had security cameras and a driveway bell, this was no longer the dogs' job. I asked them to set this up a few more times with other cars and people, and even the courier had fun helping them, as he was fed up with having to call and wait for the dogs to be put away each time he turned up.

I followed up a couple of weeks later and the lady said they have only had to do the training sessions twice more and since then the dogs have been wonderful, and they love all their new jobs.

Digging

There could be several reasons why your dog is digging.

Boredom

If your dog is just digging in random places, it could be because they do not have enough to do, they are not using their mind enough through lack of stimulation.

Solutions

Give your dog more thinking to do, get them some puzzle toys.

Take more of *their* walks and *your* walks, maybe make them shorter and more frequent.

Teach them some tricks or maybe naming their toys and hiding them around the house.

Try scatter feeding, your dog has a brain - get them to use it. Ten minutes of this a day can make a huge difference to your dog's boredom levels.

Play more games with them.

Getting them fitter is often a mistake as it will only make for a bigger challenge for you.

Escape

If the dog is digging along the fence line it is wanting to escape and that brings on a whole bigger issue because if your dog is wanting to escape, it is not getting its needs met at home. You need to be working on the pack leadership and making them feel more loved and safe.

Solution

Fill the holes with their poop and maybe add some white pepper or something with a bit more kick like hot sauce, just to get them out of the habit of digging. You will have to do a lot more of the *Attentiveness* training to make them feel safe at home.

Food

Sometimes a dog will be digging so they can eat the roots of the grass or plants. Watch when your dog digs to see what or how they are doing this.

Solution

You might need to change your dog's diet to add blended raw vegetables or give them a broccoli stalk. If they don't like that sort of thing, maybe cut it in half to start with and add fish oil or something else to make it more tasty. There is a lot of wonderful information on RAW diets online.

Bedding

Yep, some will dig because they want to sit in the hole they have dug, to keep warm or comfortable.

Solution

If this is happening, try changing their bedding or where their outside bed is situated.

Some dogs will always need to dig, so try making them a digging pit. I use a child's paddling pool with small water holes at the bottom and fill it with sawdust or sand. Let them know they can dig there by playing with them, play-digging. Now go to the grass or where they have dug before and pat it with your hand. As they put their paw on it to dig *growl*, *praise* when they look away then go back to the digging pit and play dig and have fun.

How to cross the road

A dog should never cross a road without your release word, even when they are alone.

Do Not make your dog sit and stay on the side of the road, that turns it into an obedience exercise and you will have to do it all the time. The goal of this exercise is so that when your dog comes to a road, it will naturally not want to walk on it without your release command, therefore, when you are not around it will avoid the roads. If your dog is on its own it will not sit and stay on the side of the road.

Walk up towards the road and as the dog is about to step on the road, snap the lead back and growl and then give them a fast praise when they stop. Don't forget to give them loads of smiles and show you are happy and pleased with them when they stop. Do this again several times until the dog stops and waits on its own without a command, then use your release word and walk on to the road.

The dog will soon learn that a road is not a safe place to be without you. You must also use emotion here. I want you to picture your dog getting hit by a car, yes a nasty thought, but if you do not feel urgency or panic about the road, the dog will not believe you. You now need your release word for when you want to cross the road, and make sure this is not a common word. I suggest you use a word like 'Free' or 'Zip', something you would never normally use on the side of the road. The word OK is *Not* OK as a release word as it is commonly used in everyday conversation. Such common words like this can be used at the wrong time and cause your dog to enter into a dangerous situation and get hurt.

Boundary work

Boundary areas can be:

- stay out of a particular room
- don't go past the gate
- keep out of the kitchen
- don't go on the mat in the lounge

For example, if you want your dog to stay out of the kitchen, when you walk into the kitchen and your dog follows you, with your body and voice walk towards your dog pushing it out. Do not use your hands, say loudly KITCHEN, or whatever command word you want to use. If my dog starts to go upstairs, I will just say *Kitchen* and he understands it is a place he is not to go. Then when they are back behind the line - *praise*. Do this until your dog does not step over the line. *Always* praise for good.

If you have a lifestyle block or large property, take your dog to the boundary and growl as it looks to where you do not want it to be, then praise.

Yep, it's that simple. *Growl* when they are looking at or are in the wrong place, *praise* when they are in the correct place. Keep It Super Simple

ASSESSMENT SHEET

This is just to check in to see how you are going.

Dog's Name: Age:

Breed: Today's Date:

How to rate your dog's progress:

ACHIEVEMENT LEVEL	SCORE
Absolutely Wonderful, no improvement required	5
Best efforts, just about there	4
Could have been better, understanding just no follow through	3
Did try, well ok needs to try harder	2
Effort was not really there	1
Forget it, epic fail. Come on human I do not understand	0

Dog's Training - score 1 to 5 for each action - with 5 being the highest score

ACTION SCORE

Do I look at my human's face when there is trouble or I am afraid

How is my short lead work at home

How is my short lead walk out with distractions

How is my long lead work at home

How is my long lead walk out with distractions

Putting the lead on calmly

What am I like around my human's food

Is my barking a problem

My obedience commands. Sit- stay- wait

How is my mat and/or crate training going

Am I doing well when guests arrive

Recall at home

Recall out in public with distractions

Boundary work, keep out of the kitchen, don't go out of the gate

Respond to the word "Leave"

Dog reactive

People Reactive

My reaction to loud noises

Obsessive behavior

Separation Anxiety

Vet Check by my human

Vet check by the vet

Nail clipping

Total Score

    Human Training Self Check - score 1 to 5 for each action - 5 being the highest score

ACTION   **SCORE**

Has my human done attentiveness training at least 3 times a day

Has my human praised me enough

Has my human taken me for a walk each day

Has my human seen how my focus is casually around the home

Has my human set up distraction training often enough

How is my human's breathing and calm while training

Is my human making more rules for me and sticking to them

Is my human being consistent with my training

Is my human using their emotions with their commands

Total Score

The Trainer

At the time of publication Maree has been a professional dog behavior trainer for over 27 years. For Maree, dog training is more than a job or a career, it is her life, it is who she is.

When Maree was a young girl of seven, she had her first dog, a corgi. Her corgi, the cats and the farm dog would do anything for her. Even the goats, calves and chickens were welcome to join in the fun if they wanted to. They would climb a ladder, walk on hind legs, crawl, hide, freeze on the spot and do anything else Maree asked them to. The tricks were easy because she knew how to communicate with the animals. It wasn't until she was nine that the real training began. Her Dad was given a dog and it was a bit of a *'rat bag'* as her Dad would say. This was to be her first challenge when it came to training, she knew that if she didn't train this dog properly, it would be shot, so she trained it very well.

Maree started her working life on a farm. One of her first jobs after that was as a vet nurse. Not able to handle people putting their pets to sleep because they said they were 'bad', she thought there must be a better way. Maree decided to run a boarding kennel and after about five years, watching the behavior of the dogs became a passion. She discovered that working with dogs and their humans was enormously rewarding. Then it was time to leave the boarding kennels and pursue her true passion, training. She subsequently trained with several dog trainers both in New Zealand and overseas. Most of the trainers had different ways of training and anything that would harm the dog was instantly dismissed, as Maree believed that nothing learns well when in pain or fear and besides, that just didn't sit right with her. Maree went back to the training she developed as a child where the animals would always focus on her and understand what she was expecting from them. 'Treat training' never made sense to her, she never used it and the animals would still do anything for her.

Maree has done several dog training courses over the years and is always looking at what is happening in the world of dog training. Maree found what worked with her beliefs and her caring nature. 'It is all about going back to nature, understanding your dog, using love and praise'. Over the past 27 years of training, some things have changed, and Maree is always open to learning new things, however the core of the 'respect training' has stayed the same. Dog training is more than a job, it is a passion and, as Maree will tell you, it is who she is.

All the stories in this book are an actual account of real lessons Maree has done, however, fake names have been used because she knows she would get in the shit for using the real ones.